SOCIAL ISSUES FIRSTHAND

Adoption

Other books in the
Social Issues Firsthand series:

Homosexuality
Poverty
Suicide
Terrorism

Adoption

David M. Haugen and Matthew J. Box,
Book Editors

Bruce Glassman, Vice President
Bonnie Szumski, Publisher
Helen Cothran, Managing Editor
Scott Barbour, Series Editor

GREENHAVEN PRESS
An imprint of Thomson Gale, a part of The Thomson Corporation

Detroit • New York • San Francisco • San Diego • New Haven, Conn.
Waterville, Maine • London • Munich

For more information, contact
Greenhaven Press
27500 Drake Rd.
Farmington Hills, MI 48331-3535
Or you can visit our Internet site at http://www.gale.com

Cover credit: © Landov. A nine-month-old Thai boy sits in his crib at a Bangkok orphanage in July 2002.

LIBRARY OF CONGRESS CATALOGING-IN-PUBLICATION DATA

Adoption / David M. Haugen and Matthew J. Box, book editors.
    p. cm. — (Social issues firsthand)
Includes bibliographical references and index.
ISBN 0-7377-2881-7 (lib. : alk. paper)
    1. Adoption—Case studies. I. Haugen, David M., 1969– . II. Box, Matthew J., 1976– . III. Series.
HV875.A316   2006
362.734—dc22   2005046075

Printed in the United States of America

CONTENTS

SOC

CHAPTER 1: GIVING UP A CHILD FOR ADOPTION

CHAPTER 2: CHOOSING TO ADOPT

CHAPTER 3: ADOPTEE EXPERIENCES

CHAPTER 4: SEARCHING FOR AND REUNITING WITH BIRTH MOTHERS

Social issues are often viewed in abstract terms. Pressing challenges such as poverty, homelessness, and addiction are viewed as problems to be defined and solved. Politicians, social scientists, and other experts engage in debates about the extent of the problems, their causes, and how best to remedy them. Often overlooked in these discussions is the human dimension of the issue. Behind every policy debate over poverty, homelessness, and substance abuse, for example, are real people struggling to make ends meet, to survive life on the streets, and to overcome addiction to drugs and alcohol. Their stories are ubiquitous and compelling. They are the stories of everyday people—perhaps your own family members or friends—and yet they rarely influence the debates taking place in state capitols, the national Congress, or the courts.

The disparity between the public debate and private experience of social issues is well illustrated by looking at the topic of poverty. Each year the U.S. Census Bureau establishes a poverty threshold. A household with an income below the threshold is defined as poor, while a household with an income above the threshold is considered able to live on a basic subsistence level. For example, in 2003 a family of two was considered poor if its income was less than $12,015; a family of four was defined as poor if its income was less than $18,810. Based on this system, the bureau estimates that 35.9 million Americans (12.5 percent of the population) lived below the poverty line in 2003, including 12.9 million children below the age of eighteen.

Commentators disagree about what these statistics mean. Social activists insist that the huge number of officially poor Americans translates into human suffering. Even many families that have incomes above the threshold, they maintain, are likely to be struggling to get by. Other commentators insist that the statistics exaggerate the problem of poverty in the United States. Compared to people in developing countries, they point out, most so-called poor families have a high quality of life. As stated by journalist Fidelis Iyebote, "Cars are owned by 70 percent of 'poor' households. . . . Color televisions belong to 97 percent of the 'poor' [and] videocassette recorders belong to nearly 75 percent. . . . Sixty-four percent have microwave ovens, half own a stereo system, and over a quarter possess an automatic dishwasher."

However, this debate over the poverty threshold and what it means is likely irrelevant to a person living in poverty. Simply put, poor people do not need the government to tell them whether they are poor. They can see it in the stack of bills they cannot pay. They are aware of it when they are forced to choose between paying rent or buying food for their children. They become painfully conscious of it when they lose their homes and are forced to live in their cars or on the streets. Indeed, the written stories of poor people define the meaning of poverty more vividly than a government bureaucracy could ever hope to. Narratives composed by the poor describe losing jobs due to injury or mental illness, depict horrific tales of childhood abuse and spousal violence, recount the loss of friends and family members. They evoke the slipping away of social supports and government assistance, the descent into substance abuse and addiction, the harsh realities of life on the streets. These are the perspectives on poverty that are too often omitted from discussions over the extent of the problem and how to solve it.

Greenhaven Press's Social Issues Firsthand series provides a forum for the often-overlooked human perspectives on society's most divisive topics of debate. Each volume focuses on one social issue and presents a collection of ten to sixteen narratives by those who have had personal involvement with the topic. Extra care has been taken to include a diverse range of perspectives. For example, in the volume on adoption, readers will find the stories of birth parents who have given up their children for adoption, adoptive parents, and adoptees themselves. After exposure to these varied points of view, the reader will have a clearer understanding that adoption is an intense, emotional experience full of joyous highs and painful lows for all concerned.

Each book in the series contains several features that enhance its usefulness, including an in-depth introduction, an annotated table of contents, bibliographies for further research, a list of organizations to contact, and a thorough index. These elements—combined with the poignant voices of people touched by tragedy and triumph—make the Social Issues Firsthand series a valuable resource for research on today's topics of political discussion.

Open and Closed Adoptions

In the United States an adult (or pair of adults) wishing to adopt a child can do so in a variety of ways. While some adoptive parents find their children in foreign countries such as China and former Soviet republics, about 85 percent of American adoptions are conducted within the United States. For these domestic adoptions, prospective parents can choose to adopt a child from within their community, or they can scour the network of adoption agencies across America. To arrange for an adoption, adoptive parents can choose to work with an agency (whether public or private), or they can arrange to adopt directly from a birth mother with the assistance of lawyers or an unlicensed facilitator (if state laws permit this practice). Much of this process of locating a child for adoption has not changed in the past twenty years. What has changed significantly since the 1980s, though, is the relationship among birth mothers (and sometimes birth fathers), adoptive parents, and adopted children in many domestic adoptions.

Prior to the liberalization of social norms that occurred in the 1960s and 1970s, most states had framed their adoption laws to ensure complete anonymity between birth mothers and the parents who would adopt their children. These so-called closed adoptions in theory cut the adopted child loose from his or her past so that the adoptive family could start fresh without any lingering stigma from the supposedly "unfit" parent who was forced to give up the child for adoption. After the moral tide shifted in the 1960s, the shame associated with giving up a child to adoption began to ebb, and birth mothers became more determined to take part in placing their children with parents who they felt would provide a good home. The concept of "open adoption" was born in the 1960s (although open adoptions were not practiced until the 1980s) and continued to evolve over the next two decades to encompass not only the birth mother's desire to help place her child but also her desire to maintain contact with the child throughout the child's life. Since the 1980s open adoptions have gained prominence in the United States, but many agencies still conduct closed adoptions (though few are left that exclusively offer closed adoptions). While this sea change has pleased the many advocates of open adoption who believe all parties benefit from the open arrangement, there is still controversy over the risks and rewards of choosing one form of adoption over the other.

THE ORIGINS OF CLOSED ADOPTION

Closed adoption was a creation of nineteenth-century Victorian culture. Victorian society frowned on children born out of wedlock and held in contempt the mothers who would, by necessity, have to give up such children. Medical editor and author Louann Carroll writes that those who gave birth to illegitimate or unwanted children were "labeled misfits, outcasts, bad girls, and were secretly whisked away to give birth to their children in nunnery's and secret hospitals across the nation."[1] Private and public agencies were created to take charge of the "unwanted" children. While these organizations usually had compassion for unwed mothers, they subscribed to the belief that the agency directors, not the mothers, were better suited to placing these children with prospective parents. Bruce M. Rappaport, the founder and executive director of the Independent Adoption Center, an adoption agency that facilitates open adoption, notes that, because illegitimacy was such a hushed topic, "The agencies met little resistance establishing almost total power over the adoption process by the early 1900's."[2] The agencies also initiated the first record keeping of adoptions and made the transfer of a child from birth mother to adoptive parents a legal matter. Even these records were considered tainted by the immorality of the whole issue. In 1917 Minnesota became the first state to pass a law mandating that the information about a child's history be keep sealed. By the 1950s almost every other state had amended its adoption laws to follow Minnesota's lead.

The secrecy associated with surrendering a child to adoption largely went unquestioned through the 1950s. Adoption agencies as well as state legislators believed that the interests of the children were served by keeping information about birth parents sealed. Even adoptive parents had no recourse to find out anything about the birth parents of their adopted children. Although the agencies needed adoptive parents, these Samaritans were not trusted with such information. Those looking to adopt were treated with a degree of moral scrutiny that placed them above the unfit birth mothers but still below the average, reproductive American family. As Rappaport mentions, agencies often labeled adoptive parents "barren"—a pejorative term that questioned the health and normalcy of their marriage.

THE DAWN OF OPEN ADOPTION

The questioning of social norms that defined the decades of the 1960s and 1970s led to a rethinking of the power vested in adoption agencies. Changing sexual mores removed some of the stigma associated with bearing children out of wedlock, and the female empowerment movement made birth mothers more aware of, and less afraid to use, their legal rights to be involved in choosing the parents who would care for their children. Pressure also began to surface from adopted children who had grown to adulthood during the closed adoption era and now demanded access to the parts of their past that had been sealed up in record-keeping vaults. Then in 1974 another—perhaps more influential—factor seemed to herald the need for an alternative to closed adoption. Newly published studies of adopted children, birth parents, and adoptive parents revealed that many suffered psychological problems that were in some way related to their inability to fill in all parts of their personal adoption histories because of the imposed secrecy of the closed adoption process. The children exhibited the most telling problems since many had come to believe that their biological parents had simply discarded them and then hid behind the wall of anonymity.

In the 1970s agencies in Arizona began offering to share some information about adopted children between birth parents and adoptive parents. In the next decade some states began passing laws that allowed adopted children to seek out their birth mothers, provided that both gave written consent to the exchange of information. More significantly for the adoption process, however, a few adoption agencies initiated the practice of allowing birth mothers to take part in the selection of appropriate adoptive parents for their children. Thus, as journalist Gabrielle Glaser claims, "The first open adoptions are believed to have started in California in the early 1980s."[3]

Since that time, the practice of open adoption has evolved. Birth mothers not only became involved in approving adoptive parents;

they also insisted that they be allowed to remain in contact with their children and the adoptive parents. By the end of the twentieth century, open adoption had become the standard practice, since, given the choice, fewer birth mothers opted to abandon their children with little hope of seeing them again. The vast majority relished the idea that even if they could not support their children, they could at least remain a prominent part of their children's lives.

DEFINING OPEN ADOPTION

Some champions of open adoption believe that disclosing all information about birth parents and adoptive parents is healthier for both the children and the adults involved. In their well-regarded work *Children of Open Adoption and Their Families*, Kathleen Silber and Patricia Martinez Dorner write, "Open adoption was designed to provide answers and to eliminate the myths and misunderstandings in adoption. Open adoption is also a concept in keeping with changes in society which require honesty and openness in human relationships."[4] In this appraisal, open adoption allows adopted children to know their birth mothers (and possibly their birth fathers) and therefore dispenses with false pedigrees or anxiety that these otherwise unknown birth parents had simply abandoned their children. Silber and Dorner's definition also emphasizes that today's society favors disclosure and honest communication. This ideal degree of openness, however, does not characterize every open adoption, a fact that Silber and Dorner make very clear in the introduction to their book.

As practiced in the 1980s, open adoption included any form of contact between the three parties involved in the adoption process (birth parents, adoptive parents, and adopted children). Such contact could be made directly or through an intermediary (a lawyer or agency facilitator, for example), and the forms of contact might range from an exchange of letters to face-to-face meetings. Silber and Dorner argue that this variety of contact options is too broad to be covered by the term "open adoption." Instead, they maintain that exchanging letters and photos or even meeting a few times does not characterize an open adoption; instead, such "openness" defines a "semi-open adoption." A true open adoption, on the other hand, "includes the birthparents and adoptive parents meeting one another, sharing full identifying information, and having access to ongoing contact over the years."[5]

Under Silber and Dorner's definition of open adoption, the ongoing relationship is established at birth and typically involves both parties entering into an "ongoing contact agreement." Such an agreement spells out the type of contact that will be maintained, the frequency of collective visits, and any financial arrangements that may be necessary to ensure that visits can take place. Some proponents of open adoption worry, though, that these contracts are not binding. As Louann Carroll writes, "The Ongoing Contact Agreement is simply an agreement between two parties, the birth parent and the adoptive parents, to allow informal ongoing contact. If the adoptive parents choose to change their phone number, move across country, or ignore letters from the birth mother, they can legally do so."[6] As Carroll suggests, there is nothing about the open adoption arrangement that allows for legal recourse; both parties enter into such an agreement because they commonly believe that it is in the best interests of the adopted child, but neither is under any obligation to uphold their side of the bargain.

STRENGTHS AND WEAKNESSES OF OPEN ADOPTION

Those who promote open adoption and support ongoing contact agreements claim that the arrangement benefits adopted children by providing them with a means of answering any questions they may have about their heritage. It also supposedly reduces adopted children's feelings of abandonment since the birth mothers are, from the beginning, part of their children's lives. Open adoption is also claimed to be a salve for birth parents who otherwise might harbor lingering doubt that they left their children with unfit parents. Furthermore, Silber and Dorner claim that open adoption grants birth mothers peace of mind that they have made a plan for their children's future welfare instead of merely delivering them to an unknown fate. Finally, advocates of open adoption insist that the process is beneficial to adoptive parents as well. In closed adoptions, adoptive parents may think of birth mothers as potential threats to the well-being of the new family because they might someday demand their child back. The open adoption arrangement decreases this threat because it allows the adoptive parents to establish a relationship with their child's birth mother that is based on trust that both sets of parents have made the right decision.

Open adoption is not, however, without its skeptics. As some note, the full-disclosure, ongoing-contact form of open adoption is a relatively new phenomenon, and no long-term studies have been conducted to see if the proposed rewards counter some of the problems noted in the surveys conducted in the 1970s. In an editorial to the *Kansas City Star*, John W. Dunham, an adoptee who found out about his adoption when he was older, argues that rearing a child under open adoption could be mentally straining to a young mind. "Expecting a young child to sort out issues of birth and adoptive families and relationships with both would seem—at least in some cases—very problematical," Dunham writes. "For example, should it be expected of the adoptive family to explain, when a child asks, why his birth family is able to be involved in his life on a regular basis but unable to rear him as their own?"[7]

Dunham believes that his closed adoption allowed him to mature to a point in his life at which he was able to understand adoption and have his family comfortably explain the circumstances of his own adoption to him. Until that time, Dunham asserts, his family placed emphasis "on my future instead of my origins."[8] In fact, when his adopted status was revealed, Dunham maintains that he carried with him a feeling that to seek out his birth parents would "dishonor" his adoptive parents. He claims that many other adopted individuals also believe that contacting birth parents would be a betrayal of the love that their adoptive parents have shown.

Even proponents of open adoption contend that there may be some unforeseen pitfalls along the way. Silber and Dorner, for example, state that "there can be minor differences in lifestyles and values" between birth mothers and adoptive parents that could lead to contests over child rearing. "There can also be minor relationship problems," the authors continue. "As with one's biological relatives, there are times when they may disagree with one another."[9] As Silber and Dorner's comments illustrate, those who champion open adoption typically suggest that these potential problems are "minor." Those who are skeptical of open adoption, however, argue that any conflict between birth mothers and adoptive parents can force a child to choose sides. Others simply maintain that involving birth mothers or birth parents in the child's growth will weaken the bond between the child and the adoptive family.

OPEN ADOPTION REMAINS A CHOICE

Despite the debate over the benefits and harms of open adoption, this practice is becoming the norm. In 2004 over half of the adoptions certified in the United States had some degree of openness. Rappaport predicts the trend will continue. "Today, people still talk about open and closed adoption," he states. "Within a few years, those terms will have lost their meaning. Openness will be the rule (with a few exceptions, of course) and what we now call open adoption will just be called 'adoption.'"[10] However, other observers stress the importance of honoring all forms of adoption. Louann Carroll, for example, argues that "both open and closed adoptions need to be . . . respected by all."[11] After all, closed adoptions are still conducted in the United States, sometimes at the request of the adoptive parents and sometimes by the demand of the birth mother. Furthermore, all international adoptions are closed adoptions, and the possibility of even tracing the birth mother in such adoptions varies by country. Open adoption, then, remains a choice in the broad spectrum of adoption possibilities. Whether it will truly come to characterize the concept of adoption, as Rappaport suggests, will depend on evolving social norms and beliefs about whether open adoption clearly serves the best interests of the children.

NOTES

1. Louann Carroll, "The History of Open Adoption," About.com. http://adoption.about.com/od/adoptionrights/a/historyofopen.htm.
2. Bruce M. Rappaport, "Open Adoption History," Independent Adoption Center. www.adoptionhelp.org/historyofadoption/historyof openadoption.html.
3. Gabrielle Glaser, "Open Hearts," *Oregonian*, October 24, 2004.
4. Kathleen Silber and Patricia Martinez Dorner, *Children of Open Adoption and Their Families*. San Antonio, TX: Corona, 1990, p. 7.
5. Silber and Dorner, *Children of Open Adoption and Their Families*, p. 9.
6. Carroll, "The History of Open Adoption."
7. John W. Dunham, "As I See It: Adoption—Open and Closed—Carry Strengths, Weaknesses," *Kansas City Star*, May 24, 1999.
8. Dunham, "As I See It."
9. Silber and Dorner, *Children of Open Adoption and Their Families*, p. 17.
10. Rappaport, "Open Adoption History."
11. Carroll, "The History of Open Adoption."

Giving up a Child for Adoption

SOCIAL ISSUES FIRSTHAND

Giving Up My Child Was the Right Decision

by Patty O'Keefe

Patty O'Keefe became pregnant as the result of a tryst with a man who was not willing to stay with her and help her raise a child. Without support, O'Keefe was not ready for the demands of motherhood, so she gave her baby up for adoption.

Once the choice was made, O'Keefe attests that everything worked out for the best. Through an open adoption process, O'Keefe found a suitable family that was willing to give her baby the best possible chance at being happy. Fate seemed to play a role in the union because, as O'Keefe claims, the adoptive parents had chosen a name for the child that was nearly identical to the one O'Keefe had secretly selected.

O'Keefe maintains that giving her daughter up for adoption was a difficult thing to do; however, she is convinced that she made the right decision. Through letters that she has received over the years, O'Keefe has kept apprised of her little girl's upbringing and is pleased with the results. She also says that a spiritual belief in God has helped her through the tough moments in her life since the adoption.

This October, as my first daughter's 18th birthday drew near, I was reminded of the amazing ways God works in our lives. She has grown happy, healthy and strong, and though my heart aches to know mine are not the arms that raised her, I am grateful for the guidance from God that has given her a wonderful life.

Eighteen years ago I was 20 years old and living in Spokane, Washington. Somehow, having survived an adolescence marked by alcohol and drug abuse, nevertheless, I was drifting in and out of one dysfunctional relationship after another. I did manage to complete a program to train as a dental assistant, and after breaking free from an abusive relationship, was making it on my own.

Mark and I had dated between break-ups with Kirk, and were

dating again now that I was free. When we first met, Mark was shy, sweet, and attentive, but during the few months we had been apart, he had changed. He had begun working out and had built up an amazing bulk in a short time. I noticed he was often surly and argumentative; I wasn't so sure it was going to work out.

One weekend I was feeling especially moody and just wanted to see Mark and be held. After checking with his mom, I found his pickup parked outside a bar downtown, so I went in. My stomach lurched when I saw him sitting at a table with his brother and two ladies. Sitting in the far corner, I asked the waiter to send over a beer and say it was from me. He looked up, glared at me, and went back to his conversation. I left the bar devastated, thinking, "Well, I guess that's over."

MAKING A DIFFICULT DECISION

A week or so later, the reason for my moodiness became apparent when a home pregnancy test came out positive. After the initial emotional roller coaster subsided, I knew what I had to do. You see, I had never been the kind of girl to daydream about a big wedding, kids, house-in-the-suburbs and all that stuff of fairy tales. One thing I knew in my heart was that when I did have a baby, it was going to have a mom and a dad and a roof over its head. I had learned already that life is hard enough even under the best circumstances.

If I chose to keep this baby, we would live hand-to-mouth. What about my plans to return to college? Either I had to forget them or plan to have someone else watch the baby while I worked full-time and went to school. My mom had faced so much hardship already; I couldn't bear to burden her more. None of these alternatives felt right to me.

So I made the call and set up an appointment with an adoption counselor, Nancy Johnson, who at the time worked for a Seattle-based agency. I also knew I had to tell Mark.

When I think about that phone call, I still get a knot in the pit of my stomach. When he answered, I told him there was something he should know—that I was pregnant.

After a long pause, he simply said, "I think before we talk any more I should contact my lawyer."

Any wishes I may have been harboring about a happy family or even a supportive father for the baby went out the window then and there. The moment I decided to relinquish was the moment I began to see God at work in my life. Up until then, I had never paid much attention. My family had never been regular churchgoers, so most of what I knew about God was from the occasional trip to Sunday school with a friend.

FINDING THE RIGHT FAMILY

Things started to fall into place as I reviewed synopses from a pool of prospective parents. Nancy had asked what I was looking for in a family, and my requests were simple: college educated (like my parents), and outdoorsy (like me). At first I thought it was important that the baby go to a childless couple, but then I realized that I wasn't out to do anyone a favor—the important thing was to find the right family for this baby.

That's when their synopsis arrived. It described Bob and Susan, both psychologists (helping professions! Just like I hoped to do!) and their daughter, Maya, whom they had adopted as an infant. Something in my heart told me this was the right family, especially after I received a little folder with pictures and a letter from each family member.

A quote from Bob read, "When the moon is out, all of us go outside just to see it and ourselves in the moonlight."

Nancy was happy for me and thought I had made a wonderful choice. Even better, this family was willing to exchange letters and pictures before and after placement. Although only about six months pregnant, I was beginning to experience the grief of letting my baby go, and couldn't imagine not getting word that she was growing up happy and healthy. Otherwise, I felt, I would be haunted by images of a newborn frozen in time.

Nancy, my counselor, was invaluable during the final months. She found me a family to stay with, took me to birth mom meetings, and helped me in the process of "anticipatory grief," dealing with the feelings that accompany an impending loss. I felt very close to the baby. (I had a feeling she was a girl and called her Randi Allison, the Allison after my mom, Alice, who goes by Allie). I would spend lunch hours in the park, caressing my growing belly as she kicked (and kicked!), with me crying and telling her all the hopes and dreams I had for her and for myself.

Bob and Susan were overjoyed when they learned I had chosen them. They sent a beautiful card, followed by an incredible letter. I still cry when I remember their promise to me:

- Your baby will never cry without being heard and cared for,
- will never feel fear without being held and comforted,
- and will always go to bed knowing love and happy, strong feelings.

We continued to exchange letters, getting to know each other. Although they were older than I was, the parallels in our lives were amazing. We all come from close, loving families, Sue's mom was a teacher. The fit just seemed right.

MEETING THE NEW PARENTS AND SAYING GOOD-BYE

I brought Randi Allison into the world on a Sunday afternoon, with my mom and two sisters beside me. It was incredible; what a miracle a baby is! I chose to spend time with her in the hospital, as it was important to me to get to know her before having to say good-bye.

After spending one night home in Lewiston (where I'd moved by then), Mom and I picked the baby up at the hospital and took her to Spokane. God was really busy then. He saw to it that the place we stayed was only two houses away from the temporary foster care where Randi Allison stayed until her parents arrived.

After going to court and completing the heart-wrenching process of giving up my parental rights, I was allowed to continue visiting the baby until we learned her parents were in town. We planned a meeting on neutral ground, so Mom and I checked into a hotel and waited.

Bob and Susan arrived with the baby in a beautiful wicker bassinet ("Oh," I thought, "I could never have gotten something that cute for her"). After initial introductions between Bob, Susan, Mom and myself, Bob and Susan exchanged meaningful glances. They explained that on the plane ride over, they had been discussing baby names. They had decided on either Katie or Alyson, and if they chose Alyson they would call her "Ali." When they met my mom, Allie, they felt it was meant to be.

We spent two hours visiting, with them telling us about themselves, how they felt children should be raised, and how infertility had been difficult for them but they were overjoyed with their adopted children. My mom and I tried to fill them in on all the things adopted kids often don't know—ethnic background, family history, family talents, etc.

The end of that visit was the most painful moment of my life. I'll never forget her little sleeping self in that bassinet with red quilted lining, thankfully oblivious to the terrible pain in my heart. The next few weeks passed in a blur of tears. I had no idea I would love her so much, miss her so deeply! My mom, although grieving herself, was a rock for me. Gradually, as I returned to work, then college, time eased my pain. Birthdays continue to be emotional times, especially this one, the 18th.

My experience with Ali proved to be a turning point in my life. Through it I learned to listen to God by finding what feels right in my heart and by trying to be aware of when He is opening doors for me. Oh, I've stumbled a few times (my first marriage ended in divorce), but have arrived at a place in life where I feel He means me to be, blessed with a loving husband, two great kids, and a rewarding career as a registered nurse.

The letters I received through the years gave me peace of mind that the Lord truly guided me in the decision to give Alyson up to Bob and Susan. I don't know how she feels about me, if she's curious at all, or wants to meet me (I hope she does). All I know is that in my prayers I ask God to send her my love, always.

I Was Forced to Give Up My Child

by Glen Frazer

Prior to the 1980s, traditional adoption was a process shrouded in secrecy. Since having children out of wedlock carried a more profound social stigma, the prevalent thinking among adoption agencies at the time was that keeping information about birth mothers secret was a way to protect adopted children and their new parents from the taint of illegitimacy. In addition, because society also frowned upon single parenthood in previous decades, many mothers who gave their children up in these "closed" adoptions have recently come forward with horror stories of doctors and agency representatives badgering them into relinquishing their children to "more suitable" parents.

In the narrative that follows, Glen Frazer relates her experiences in surrendering her daughter to an agency under the terms of a closed adoption. Frazer claims she got pregnant at a young age and was immediately sent away to a hospice for unwed mothers—a practice that is atypical today. It was there, Frazer claims, that she and several other mothers-to-be were bombarded with rhetoric from counselors that argued against keeping the children. Frazer says that she and others were made to feel that it was not possible to provide a good quality of life for their unborn children because the mothers were mostly unwed and jobless. As a result, Frazer believes that she was coerced into making a decision she would not otherwise have made had she been more informed of her choices and prospects.

In hindsight, and after having and keeping a second daughter three years later, Frazer says she recognizes the importance of choosing to raise a child regardless of all the hardships one might face in doing so. She believes that if a mother gives a child love and tenderness, the child will, in return, give the mother the strength to overcome the trials of parenting.

Since the 1980s, the closed adoption process has been revamped, and "open" adoptions are growing in popularity. In the

Glen Frazer, "We Were Told We Only Wanted a Doll to Dress Up and Play With," www.exiledmothers.com, 2003. Copyright © 2003 by First Mothers Action. Reproduced by permission of the author.

open adoption process, birth parents and adoptive parents are known to each other, and the birth parents are more often in regular contact with the adoptive parents and the child as he or she grows up.

This is my story. I became pregnant at 16. I was sent out of town, to a home for unwed mothers, until the problem was taken care of. I never went home again. I was deprived of my family, my friends, my cat, my clothes, my bed, my music, and my books. In the home we were expected to attend mass every morning and "counseling" every day. If we didn't show up they came and found us and "counseled" us right where they found us.

The counseling consisted of making a list of what we could and could not give our child. The one and only thing we could give our child that no one else had, was our love. That however was negated when they told us we were too immature to love as evidenced by the fact we were pregnant. We were told we didn't know anything about child rearing (a skill that can be learned and mentored). We were told we only wanted a doll to dress up and play with (we had outgrown dolls and were baby-sitting brothers or sisters, cousins, and neighbors' kids). We were told we were selfish (people who want what you have and you won't give it up call you selfish). We were told we would deprive the baby of a decent home (backyard, picket fence, dog, two cars in the garage, the American dream) and a two parent family (normal people susceptible to disruption, job loss, divorce, bankruptcy, alcohol and drug abuse, anger, violence, poor judgement).

Counseling consisted of telling us we had nothing to offer our child and all that we would do to harm our child and every thing we would lose if we kept our child. We were told we would ruin our lives and our child's life. We were told we couldn't attend school with a baby (there are now child-care centers on campuses). We were told no one would hire a single mom (single moms work all the time, everywhere their skills and talents allow them). And we were told no decent man would be interested in a ready-made family or would want to raise another man's child (decent stepfathers and happy, healthy stepchildren are everywhere).

Nothing was ever said of the basic human survival instinctual needs an infant has for her mother. An infant is hardwired to find her favorite smell, sound, taste, feeling, and her favorite thing; her mother. When her needs are not met, when she does not connect to the rest of herself, her complete self, she becomes afraid, frustrated, and angry. She screams and cannot be consoled. Her very survival is jeopardized. An infant fresh from her universe and thrust into the world does not understand separation from herself; her complete self; her mother. She is seeking to return to the bliss of her mother, her smells, sounds, touch and taste. Bliss and euphoria are denied, safety and security are denied, and a vital connection is not made when she is denied her mother. A wounding has happened. A wound that remains open and raw until that connection is made. She is anticipating the one and only connection that can heal her wound. She searches for the one and only connection that can complete her, make the connection, the connection to the rest of herself. The connection with her mother.

The first five years of a child's life are when the child's personality is formed and when life skills are learned. In her first five years the child is the center of her own universe, the sun revolves around her. People exist only in her presence; they don't exist outside her world. Everything happens because of her. This is when she learns how to define the loss of her mother. The child's development forms her concept of what happened. Once you, her mother, are gone your child takes care of herself. She defines her world in the only way the developmental process allows her. She was abandoned because she is unlovable, she is defective and the fault lies within her. As she then passes into the next phase of development she tries to find her place in relation to the world. She is now able to verbalize her thoughts and feelings. Are those my "real" cousins? Where is my "real" mom? I don't look like you, who do I look like, laugh like? Through all of this the people who adopt, who claim your child as their own, believe they have a blank slate. They do not acknowledge the earliest experiences of your child. They do not know how to deal with the trauma of separation and the loss of mother and bliss and connection. They try to replace what was lost and cannot because they are not what was lost. Your child will search for what she has lost. When the search becomes too painful to bear, a coping mechanism will protect your child by placing her needs and her search in a dark corner, unseen and yet still there.

THE IMPORTANCE OF BEING INFORMED

At 16 and 17, I was as naive and as mature as any teenager can be. I trusted and believed adults and authority figures. I believed these people were only interested in my health and well being and the health and well being of my child. Yet these people I looked to, to take care of me, failed to teach me and prevented me from learning about child birth, child care, job skills, and government assistance. I went through my pregnancy not knowing what was happening or what to expect. I went through labor and delivery without anyone with me other than a nurse that called me derogatory names and was rough and disrespectful. My water was broken, I was sedated, no anesthetic given for a large episiotomy, and forceps were used on my daughter to pull her out. Labor and delivery was forced and fast. I was denied access to my daughter after her birth. I was frightened for my daughter and myself. When the papers were brought in to release my daughter into the care of the agency I refused. My decision was to raise my own child, where was she, bring her to me. I was told I had made my bed I was to now lie in it. It made absolutely no difference what I wanted and needed and what my daughter wanted and needed. The medical community worked with the Church, the government and an agency to deprive me of my child. I did not give my "permission." I signed a paper that told me it was done.

[Talk show psychologist] Dr. Phil [McGraw] advises women not to deprive their children of their mother. He further advises them to take care of themselves so they can give their children their mother. What do you need to do to provide your child her mother? Some things that may be of concern to you: college, employment, single parenthood, daycare, dead end jobs, state money, child support, misery for your daughter and you. Don't take the victim's part of helpless, hopeless and misery. Instead use the strength of the mother you will be for your daughter. Search out and use those services that were designed to help you parent your child. Put your pride aside so that your daughter might have the bliss she needs. Services are designed to enable you to be self sufficient. Services are temporary just as your situation is now temporary. What is permanent is that you are the mother of your daughter. She wants and deserves nothing less than her mother. Her world is you. To lose you will tear her world apart. No amount of money or things can fill the void you will leave. No father is necessary for her health and well being. What is necessary is that she makes the connection with her mother and maintain that life sustaining energy. Where can you be in five years knowing that you are all that your daughter needs and wants? Would you give your life for your child, will you better yet give your life to your child?

COMPETING INTERESTS

Regarding the lawyer, agency, counselor and couple. They will encourage you to not parent your child. They don't want you to parent your child. Do you have information with which to make a fully informed decision between parenting and not parenting your child? That is part of being informed. When you tell them you have decided to not parent your child they are wonderful and sweet and you believe they are putting your feelings and desires first, they are warm and loving. In meeting the couple two or three times you will see only part of them, the good deserving part they want you to see. Ask them how they problem solve, what they disagree or bicker or fight about. Have they grieved their inability to have a child of their own? They will give a large amount of money to the agency? And the counselor takes a salary from the agency. Of course they aren't buying your child, that would be illegal. To avoid the appearance of buying and to avoid a couple having to give an agency or lawyer a large amount of money that could otherwise be used for a child, surrender your child to a county agency. When you tell them you have decided to parent your own child what will they do? They will be disappointed and mad at you. They will, however, go on to another mother and her child. They will accept any child. Their life will not end if they don't get your daughter. However, should they get your daughter her life, as she knows it, will end and so will yours.

THE AFTERMATH

I now want to tell you the rest of my story. At 19 I again became pregnant. Her father and I had lived together a year in a small very cute apt with a cat, a lawn, friendly neighbors and lots of kids (no picket fence). He went back to his wife several months after our daughter was born. We have seen him on one occasion since then when she was 3. We were on welfare for a few years while I went to school. I accepted books and tuition from EOP [Educational Opportunity Programs, a low-income support group in California] and a BEOG [Better Educational Opportunity Grant] and food stamps and medical help. I had an after-school job with the recreation department with my daughter at my side. And I had a summer job life-guarding with my daughter in the pool all summer and lots of kids for her to play with. I met a decent, wonderful man who would meet my daughter at the Head Start bus and walk her across campus where I would meet them at the end of class. When she graduated from Head Start she then went to a pre-school program at the elementary school across the street from the college. I then attended a vocational school for eighteen months and graduated with a nursing license. We were then off welfare. We continued to get court ordered child support directly from his paycheck until my daughter was 18. We received more money from child support than welfare. When my daughter started high school I deposited the check in her account for her own use. She spent a year in New Zealand as a foreign exchange student. Using her own money she bought her own car and paid for gas and insurance herself. She now owns her own house. She drives a fire truck for a living following in the footsteps of that decent wonderful man who has been in her life from the age of 3.

I still have a very large hole in my heart from the loss of my first daughter. She is so angry with me for abandoning her she cannot have any form of communication with me. I absolutely refused to let them have my second daughter. These two young women are the absolute loves of my life. One daughter is at the greatest depths of my pain and sorrow, the other the center and greatest joy of my life.

When you decide to raise your child and give your child her mother, things will come to you to strengthen you. You and your daughter will have bliss and great joy.

I wish you all the best, I know there is a bright future out there and it includes your daughter. It was there for us.

How I Lost My Daughter and Then Found Her Again

by Adrienne Jonas

In the following narrative retired Levi Strauss worker Adrienne Jonas tells her story of giving up a daughter for adoption and, later, finding the girl and reentering her life.

Born in London but living in the United States, Jonas became pregnant in 1959 by a man she had only recently met. The man decided against entering into wedlock with Jonas, leaving her with a difficult decision to make. Because Jonas was not yet a U.S. citizen, she did not qualify for any assistance from state or federal agencies. Knowing that she would be poorly suited to take care of a child, she chose to give her baby over to an adoption agency once it had been born.

Jonas was a mother for only five days—the time it took for her to recuperate from the strains of birth. She did not see her daughter again for twenty-five more years. Once she reestablished contact, her attempts to reenter her daughter's life did not go smoothly, however. Jonas explains that it took a few more years and the birth of a granddaughter to bring Jonas and her daughter closer together.

Adrienne Jonas now lives in San Francisco where she enjoys doing volunteer work for several local organizations and is an avid participant in SeniorNet, an online volunteer organization that stresses the importance of computer literacy and communication skills among adults fifty years of age and older. Jonas's story is taken from the SeniorNet Web site.

I am originally from England, and emigrated first to Canada in 1955 and then to the U.S. in 1957. I went back to England in 1958 and returned to San Francisco in February 1959 and went out again

Adrienne Jonas, "A Birth Mother's Story," www.seniornet.org, August 11, 2001. Copyright © 2001 by SeniorNet. Reproduced by permission.

with a man I'd met and fallen for before my trip home. We were together one night and it resulted in my becoming pregnant. . . .

The man went back and forth about whether or not he would
marry me, as in those days it was not acceptable to be an "unwed
mother." Suffice to say he didn't marry me, and I had to make the
very difficult decision to do what I thought was best for my child,
and that was give it up for adoption.

I did not tell my family of my situation as I did not want to bring
shame and disgrace upon them (how things have changed—today
famous stars go out and deliberately get pregnant).

LOOKING FOR ASSISTANCE

At the time I was an alien, and no welfare or assistance was available to aliens (unlike now). There was no such thing as "food
stamps"—they didn't come along until the 60s . . . and there was no
such thing as medical coverage for pregnancy. As someone once
said to me at the time, you have 9 months to save up.

I went to the church (he was Catholic), the synagogue (I am
Jewish), Family Welfare Agency and the Jewish Family Welfare
Agency . . . all of whom said there was nothing they could do—oh,
one said that I could get aid to dependent children once the child
was born, but it amounted to about $40 a month only—not enough
for either of us to live on.

I was fortunate in my job as a secretary, in that they allowed me
to stay working until a few weeks before I gave birth (in those days
many companies made you quit working as soon as you "showed,"
especially if you met the public). They agreed also to hold my job for
me, though I wasn't sure I wanted to return as I didn't know how I
was going to face everyone, however my boss convinced me it
would be o.k. That meant I was only out of work and getting no pay
for two months. It was a struggle nevertheless. I had one decent maternity outfit, and was given a couple of skirts and blouses and a
couple of pairs of pants by a friend who had recently given birth. I
can hardly believe now that I went through about 5 months with so
few outfits, but you do what you have to do.

My doctor sent me to another doctor who specialized in fertility
treatments, and if people were still not able to get pregnant he became an intermediary with finding people such as me that were not
able to keep their babies—and then with a lawyer it was all
arranged beforehand. They paid my medical bills and the hospital—

but I did not receive any money, nor did I want any. . . . The adoption still went through the state and was completely legal.

A MOTHER FOR FIVE DAYS

When the time came to give birth I went to the hospital alone in a taxi in the early morning, about 8:00 A.M., scared and unsure. I was in a Catholic hospital and I can remember one nurse, a little plump, who was my tranquilizer!! I will not go into details of the difficulties but just say that eventually I was given a spinal (didn't have any idea of how dangerous they were) and gave birth to a 7 lb. 9 oz. daughter at 1:45 A.M. the next morning, December 23rd 1959.

I used to go and look through the glass at her in the nursery every day, until one day they stopped me in the hallway and told me to go back to my room as the adoptive parents were there to pick up the baby. She was 5 days old. I stayed in the hospital for 2 more days, going home just in time for New Year's with nothing to celebrate.

When I signed the final papers at 6 months, the Agency asked me if I would like to know what name the adoptive parents had given my daughter (I had given her a name but I knew they would not use that name), and they would not cover up the names of the adoptive parents when I had to sign, so I saw that too. None of it was ever written down but it remained in my mind all those years.

As the years went by I would think of my daughter and wonder how she was, what she was doing, what she looked like. Christmas time was particularly hard as it is a time for children—and I never did marry and have other children to take care of. When she would have been a teenager I would read about car accidents with teens and hope and pray that it wasn't her and always heaved a sigh of relief when I didn't see her name.

REESTABLISHING CONTACT

Once my daughter reached 21, I wanted to open the doors for her to find me if she wanted to (and how I hoped she did). I first went to a lawyer who was no help. I contacted the doctor who delivered her (who I still went to) and they gave me the name of the fertility doctor, but they would not give me any information. I then joined an organization that helps adopted children find their birth parents, and birth parents to find their children.

It didn't take long, and I "found" her when she was 22. I was scared to death of what would happen next. Without going into details, I sent a telegram as I didn't have a phone number and asked her to call my number. The day her new husband called was the day that I had just lost a very dear friend and former neighbor, so was not prepared for the call. However I tried to explain who I was and what I was contacting them about, but my daughter got upset, her husband threatened to call the police on me and such, and I cried too—but managed to ask him to contact my search counsellor who could better explain.

I am so very thankful that he did. After that we had no verbal communication and I would write letters to my daughter, send her cards when I went away, sent birthday gifts, and just wrote as if she answered. Then I started getting cards from her, but suddenly they stopped and I didn't know why.

THE FIRST MEETING

About 3 years later at work I received a phone call from a man who said he was a friend of my daughter. My first reaction was "is she o.k., what happened"—and found out that she had been divorced, this was a new friend, and she had told him about me so he felt we should meet. We arranged a time and place as he was taking her to dinner in the City for her 25th birthday. I went to wait at a friend's house for his call—which didn't come, so at 10:00 P.M. I went home in tears.

At around 11:00 P.M. I got the call—and we met around midnight in the lobby of the St. Francis Hotel, and my girlfriend came with me. I was scared to death—and when I saw my daughter we hugged and I burst into tears . . . so there was a role reversal for a minute—she trying to calm me down and tell me it was o.k. We all sat and had drinks, and I have a beautiful photograph of the two of us taken that night in spite of my tears!!

MEETING THE BIRTH FATHER

It was at this point that I decided it was time to tell my family and friends of my secret. My Mother was upset that I hadn't felt I could tell them at the time, but all the family were very kind and accepting of the situation. My daughter was always very curious about her birth father, so one of the things I did was take her to meet him as I knew where he worked. He knew that I had found her, but I did not tell him we were coming as I knew he wasn't able to face reality sometimes, and would not be there—so I went to the bar where he worked and told him I had someone outside that wanted to meet him—and really left him no choice.

He seemed genuinely pleased to meet her and I am glad she met him. It was important for her. He was going to cook dinner for us all at my house a few weeks after that—but of course when I went to pick him up he wasn't there and he never did see his daughter again.

BECOMING A GRANDMOTHER

So for a time we had a "neutral" friendship—but then she decided that there was no room in her life for me—and she would never, ever tell her adoptive parents that we had been in touch. This was heart-breaking for me, but I had to respect her wishes. Nevertheless I still sent her cards and letters even though she didn't reply for the longest time—but then I would get Christmas cards, and one day she wrote and told me she was getting married again (no, not to the man that brought us together) and would send me pictures, which she did.

Then in October '93 she wrote me she was expecting a baby in November and my lovely granddaughter was born. My daughter then agreed that I could come and see her, which I did when she was just 18 days old. It was storming terribly, the kind of day I wouldn't normally drive if I could help it, but nothing was going to keep me from this . . . so 9 years after I first met my daughter I was to see her again. I was very nervous but it went well and I was able to hold my grandchild. I was bursting with joy and happiness—and enjoying an experience I could only dare to dream about over all those years.

A GROWING RELATIONSHIP

When my granddaughter was almost two I took them both to England to visit my Mother and other family members and everyone was very welcoming and pleased to meet them. In the years that have followed we have had a rocky relationship—some ups and downs. Her adoptive mother developed Alzheimer's and has passed away, and now her adoptive father is suffering from dementia. My daughter got a divorce after about 3 years, but since then she has married a man she has known for many years, and who is very good and kind to her and her daughter.

They are looking after the father too. I was lucky enough to go to the wedding, and my daughter had a corsage for me to wear. I was thrilled to be made to feel a part of it all. I try to see them every month or so, and am enjoying watching my granddaughter grow into a little lady. She has become curious and asks questions, and I answer honestly anything she wants to know. So I think we are finally on the right road and it is my hope that our relationship continues to grow. I hope, too, that I can take them again to England, maybe next year.

Fighting to Regain Custody of My Son

by Erik L. Smith

In the narrative that follows, Erik L. Smith, a paralegal in Ohio, tells his story of being the birth father of a child given up for adoption in the early 1990s. Smith makes it clear that while he and his then-girlfriend agreed on adoption as an alternative to being parents, the process did not work out the way he had expected.

According to Smith, he and his partner separated shortly after she became pregnant. They had both agreed to stay in contact with one another so as to make the adoption process go smoothly. However, Smith says that he waited for several months to hear from his ex-girlfriend, and when he had had no contact with her by the due date of the baby, he began to get very suspicious. Smith eventually discovered that the woman he had impregnated had gone ahead with the adoption and told the agency that she and her baby had been abandoned by the father. Smith says he also found out that he had lost his paternity rights because he failed to respond to a suit filed by the birth mother.

Having been unfairly treated, Smith states that he decided to fight to regain custody of the child, a boy, already situated in a home with adoptive parents. Smith's narrative details some of the nasty litigation and emotional ups and downs that he underwent during the custody battle. The end result, says Smith, was an arrangement whereby the adoptive parents retained custody of the boy while allowing Smith liberal contact with his son.

Erik L. Smith works in the law office of the Columbus, Ohio-based firm Manning & Farrell. He has also written several articles for various publications concerning the legal rights and responsibilities of birth fathers.

Excluding birthfathers from the adoption process subjects adoptive parents to serious legal and emotional risks. Adoption attorneys have stated that many contested adoptions result from birthfathers feeling angry at being treated as if they didn't exist. Thus, professionals advise that one best avoids disrupted adoptions by treating birthfathers with respect from the outset.

I can vouch for this.

In 1992, my girlfriend became pregnant. Initially shocked and confused, we weren't sure what to do. Realizing neither one of us made much money and that we were not marriage material, we decided on adoption. Because the birthmother wanted to conceal the pregnancy from her parents, she moved across country where she secured a full-time teaching job with good maternity benefits. Before she left, I told her I would respect her privacy, but would like to be included in the adoption process. She agreed. She declined my offers of support money, saying she had enough funds to relocate and a good job to go to. She would call me with updates. Our dating relationship was over.

During the months that followed, I envisioned receiving a letter stating I had been named as the father of a child relinquished for adoption, that the adoption agency wanted my input about the type of couple I would like my child to be placed with, and perhaps my release of relevant medical information.

NO CONTACT

It never happened. By the due date for the birth, the mother had not called me for a month. When three more weeks went by without word, I feared abortion or baby-selling. When another week went by and I could not locate the birthmother, I knew something was amiss. Frantic and fearful, I borrowed two thousand dollars from friends and family to pay for investigators and long distance phone calls and began searching. Two months later, a lawyer located the adoption file and mailed me the documents. When I read the petition—"the unknown father has voluntarily, and with knowledge of the pregnancy, abandoned the mother"—I was befuddled. When I saw the publication notice stating that the unknown father had been "sued," I became angry. When I saw a "father information sheet" left almost blank, and a court order stating that the parental rights of the unknown father were forever terminated, I was furious.

What had transpired was obvious. My ex-girlfriend had gone to an adoption agency claiming she did not know who the child's father was. Making no practical inquiry, the agency presented the scant evidence to a judge who, seeing no problem with it, placed my son with adoptive parents who thought it worth the gamble.

CUSTODY BATTLE

I borrowed ten thousand more dollars from my family to pay for a lawyer, who filed a motion for new trial, demanding my son be given to me. The agency and the adoptive parents refused, questioning my motivations. Did I really care about the child? Or was I feeling rejected by the mother, or spiteful at being left out?

The answer was all of the above. I had always cared about my son and his future. That was why I had wanted a say in the adoption—because I cared. But I was also angry. Very angry. Being lied about made me angry. Being left out made me angry. Being discarded for the interests of others made me angry. "Fit parent" and "ignoring the parental rights of others" were, to me, mutually exclusive concepts. In short, I did not feel my son was born in sin. But I felt he was living amongst it. What happened from then on only served, in my mind, to prove it.

The adoptive parents and the adoption agency filed briefs, alleging that I was mentally ill and, though I was now known, had abandoned the child and birthmother. They hired investigators to interview my friends, employers, co-workers, and acquaintances. At least twenty depositions ensued. I was deposed for twenty-four hours over four days, during which I was grilled on the use of diapers, the prices of baby clothes and formula, my past addresses for ten years, every job I had ever had, the dates I had had sex with the birthmother, my phone records, past girlfriends, past lawsuits, and more. They sought my medical records for the last eight years, and all psychological records for my life, though I could easily prove I had no record of drug abuse, physical violence, mental illness, criminal activity, or sexual predation. It struck me that an ounce of investigation before the placement would have avoided the ton of investigation now.

Nine months into the process, the court appointed an *ad litem* for my son. The *ad litem* conceded that my due process had been violated, but that my son should stay with the adoptive parents because so much time had passed, and because I could not support him. In other words, I was supposed to "see the light," and recognize that the child's interests demanded he stay with the adoptive parents, that I could not possibly raise my son all by myself, and that the adoptive parents were innocent victims. Why couldn't I see through my anger and be realistic and reasonable? It was time to start "thinking about the child."

TORMENT FOR ALL INVOLVED

It didn't work that way. Why? Because my trust in everyone associated with this adoption was gone. I had respected the birthmother's privacy and refrained from interfering with her life, only to be taken advantage of. I had been dumb in public, but I was not an abandoner. The other parties were wrongly telling my son that the man who brought him into this world had not cared about him. The only one I trusted now was me. If that meant prolonging my torment then so be it.

But I wasn't the only one tormented. The adoptive parents were devastated. When we met privately to "talk things through" no more than a few minutes went by before they started crying. "He's the center of our lives—it would kill him to take him away." Due apparently to rage, the adoptive mother did not want to see or communicate with the birthmother. But at hearing recesses, the adoptive father, dabbing at tears, would approach her. "We love this child very much, and he's such a happy little boy. We're just trying to do what's best for him." The birthmother would stand there feeling guilty and helpless.

At the trial, the adoptive mother arrived clutching a large photograph of my son, apparently a plea for us and the court to consider who really mattered. I appreciated seeing my son's picture. But what I, and likely everyone else, mostly saw were the signs of an impending breakdown on the face of the woman holding it.

The legal expenses were staggering. By the hearing on the motion for new trial, my son almost a year old, the adoptive parents' attorney fees were a rumored seventy thousand dollars. By trial, they testified to over a hundred thousand dollars. They also had to make expensive plane trips for the hearings, while leaving the child with others. The adoptive father exhausted his vacation benefits. The couple took a second mortgage out on their home. Their court briefs continually mentioned the emotional impact the litigation was having on their home life—their dreams were dashed, they were living in prolonged, constant fear for the child's future, and this was complicating their relationship with him. They had waited for years to adopt a child, and finally their dream had come true.

Their love for this human being was equal to that of any biological parent. They wanted to end this nightmare as soon as possible.

Attempts at mediation were futile. The adoptive parents and I were brick walls, our self-serving echoes drowning out reason:

Can't you see ours is the only home this child has ever known?

It's not his home I'm worried about. He's my child.

Biology isn't what's important.

It was important before you had two miscarriages.

We're not trying to keep you out of your son's life.

That's not what your court documents say—why didn't the agency investigate more?

Why didn't you come forward, you knew more than we did? You sat around during the whole pregnancy doing nothing.

He's my son, you know I did not abandon him, now give him back.

That wouldn't be in his best interests, he's our son too, can't you see we just want to do what's best for him?

And on and on.

AN AGREEMENT

On the day of trial, completely out of finances, seeing no end in sight, my son going on two years old, I offered to enter a legal custody agreement with the adoptive parents. The adoption would be set aside and the agency would pay my attorney fees and expenses. The adoptive parents would retain custody, while I got liberal visitation. Anything less and we would go to trial. Everyone accepted the offer. It remains unchanged today.

But why did it have to go that way, when a simple showing of respect and understanding would have given all an informed choice at the outset, a chance to avoid the destructive litigation, abusive investigations, a quarter of a million dollars in total legal expenses, and eighteen months of deep grief for fear of losing a child we loved?

Choosing to Adopt

SOCIAL ISSUES FIRSTHAND

Choosing to Adopt Older Children

by Kate Robertson

Freelance writer Kate Robertson relates in the narrative that follows how she and her husband Kevin came to adopt two older children. She explains that the decision came on the heels of several unsuccessful attempts to have a child of their own. Finally choosing to adopt, the Robertsons examined the various alternatives, such as adopting a foreign baby or adopting an infant from a private agency. In the meantime, they decided to become foster parents while trying to figure out the best way to build a family. As surrogate parents, the Robertsons began to realize the importance of helping older children, who, as Robertson argues, have a harder time finding homes. She says that such children commonly have emotional problems and behavior difficulties that make them less desirable to adopt than infants. As a result of their experience as foster parents, the couple decided to adopt two older children. While Robertson concedes that adopting and raising older children is not without its challenges, she argues that the rewards are worth any pains.

Kate Robertson is a former managing editor of *Island Scene Online*, a health and culture web journal focused on the Hawaiian Islands. Robertson wrote the following piece for *Island Scene* while living in Louisiana. She and her husband have since relocated to Texas, where the pair have a growing family that now includes four adopted children.

We thought we wanted a baby. A tiny fist wrapped around our fingers. The smell of talcum powder, fabric softener and baby lotion. A coo, a cry, a cuddle.

But after months of trying to conceive—including an unsuccessful attempt at in vitro fertilization—my husband, Kevin, and I decided to explore other options.

Some neighbors of ours in Honolulu had adopted a baby girl

from China. A cousin adopted a baby through a private adoption agency. And then there were the many Russian babies in the orphanages we'd heard so much about.

Because of the close proximity to the East and the strong Asian influence in Hawaii, a lot of Island residents choose foreign adoption, says Linda Santos, director of the Casey Family Program, a private agency that places local children in foster and adoptive homes.

But before Kevin and I could decide what to do, he was offered a promotion that moved us to the Mainland. After settling into our new home in New Orleans, we again began weighing our options.

It wasn't long before we decided to wade into parenting by signing up to be foster parents. We thought we could help a child while trying to figure out the best way to get one of our own. We imagined a toddler, dirty-faced and hungry, delivered to our door, longing to be loved and nurtured.

That's not what happened.

SPECIAL NEEDS

As in Hawaii, Louisiana couples who want to become certified foster or adoptive parents must take a nine-week course where you learn a lot about parenting and a lot about the children who need homes.

The faces of orphan children look remarkably the same in every state. They are 6 and 10 and 12. They are children with difficult histories, even horrors. They are not blank slates. They are not infants or toddlers. And they aren't eager to move into your home.

They have emotional problems and learning disabilities and perhaps even serious health concerns. But like all children, they need forever families. A place to call home, a place of safety and guidance today, a place to bring the grandkids for Christmas tomorrow.

Hawaii adoption agencies have seen a recent increase in the number of infants available for adoption, Santos says. That's primarily due to a more aggressive approach by the state to remove children more quickly from dangerous homes. But babies are usually easy to place. Young couples—many from the Island's large military population—yearn for babies.

It's the older children who have a harder time finding a home.

"We have a real need for families for all types of children," says Tonia Mahi, an adoption supervisor with the Department of Human Services in Hawaii. "But children with special needs, older children and those with siblings are usually the hardest to place."

And so before we even finished the foster-parenting course, Kevin and I knew what we wanted. We wanted to create a family with special-needs children.

It didn't take long for our children to find us. One of the class instructors was the temporary foster mother of a sister and brother, ages 8 and 10, who were not yet available for adoption, but were expected to be shortly and therefore needed an adoptive family. We saw their pictures, arranged for a weekend visit and three weeks later our family grew by two.

SPECIAL FIRSTS

Those first few days were a bit uncomfortable for us all. Kevin and I were excited and happy to be foster parents and tried hard to help the children settle into their rooms and into the family. They were polite houseguests, busy with the business of starting a new school and picking out new clothes and toys. The process of becoming a true family unfolded in the months to come.

Couples who consider adopting older children often worry that they will mourn having missed the many firsts associated with the formative years: First step, first word . . . first grade.

But parents of older adopted children have their own special set of firsts. The first time my son, Derek, stopped calling me "Miss Kate" and called me Mom. And how he apparently liked the sound of it, and for the next few days liberally sprinkled every sentence with it.

"Mom, what's for dinner, Mom? Oh, and Mom, can I go outside to play, Mom?"

Or the first time my daughter, Arielle, blurted out "I love you" as she ran off to catch the school bus.

Or the first time my son felt safe enough to whisper in my ear a painful secret—a hurt he'd never told anyone—trusting that I would help him heal.

Or the first time someone passed by my desk at work, noticed the many photographs of the children and knowing nothing of my family's history asked, "Are those your kids?" And I said, "Yes, yes they are."

SPECIAL CHALLENGES

Are there challenges you wouldn't have with birth children? Absolutely. Our children, like most adopted children, have special needs resulting from the tremendous loss they experienced moving from the home of their birth parents, to homes of various relatives, to foster homes and finally to our home. Their home.

We have had some behavior problems, anger outbursts and nightmares. But we have also had plenty of laughter, love and a growing trust.

Another challenge faced by adoptive families of older children is the birth family. In our case, a teenaged brother and maternal grandparents who the children adore; and an aunt and uncle who are temporarily holding up our adoption of the children as they wage a legal battle with the state over custody—an honor they abused and lost long ago.

Each day we journey into uncharted waters and we find ways to bring some members of the birth family into the fold of our family and all the while act as sentry against those who can only do damage. . . .

Derek and Arielle now have a home. And as I walk with my children, their small hands in mine, their smell of strawberry shampoo and Sweet Tarts, I cuddle them close and I know I have the babies I was meant to have. And so we wait as the adoption moves forward, waiting for a judge to say what we already know: We are a family.

Finding a Child on the Other Side of the World

by Laurie Landry

Laurie Landry is a former research assistant for Cornell University's Department of Plant Breeding; she is now a stay-at-home mom. In the following narrative Landry tells how she and her husband, Roger, decided to adopt a Chinese baby.

Landry claims that the couple was undecided about what type of adoption would best suit their desire to have a family until they attended a seminar given by the New Life Adoption Agency in Syracuse, New York. The agency, while providing myriad adoption options, specializes in joining American parents with children born in China. Encouraged by the seminar, Landry and her husband soon agreed to undertake an international adoption.

Landry's narrative provides a detailed account of the process that she and Roger underwent from the instant they decided to adopt, through their travels to Guangzhou, China, to the moment they returned to the United States with their newly acquired Chinese daughter. She tells of the culture shock that the couple experienced at being transplanted in a foreign land, the stress of having a great deal to do in a short amount of time, and the reactions of Guangzhou citizens to the adoption of Chinese children by American parents. While the experience was exhausting, according to Landry, she and Roger have since been accepted for a second visit to China in order to adopt another child.

L ike many couples, our story starts with many years of trying to conceive, visiting doctors, and undergoing fertility tests and procedures. All of this was complicated by the fact that we were constantly on the move, changing cities and states frequently as Roger and I pursued our careers. In retrospect, I guess what we were doing was slowly working our way toward our decision to adopt—we just needed to settle down in one spot long enough to start our family! When we moved to Ithaca, NY, we decided the time was right. Compared to the length of time it took us to realize this, our choice of adopting a baby from China came quickly.

We started from scratch, neither of us having any preconceptions about what kind of adoption we would want. I did research into different types of adoption, domestic vs. international, infant vs. older child, which agencies, etc., and then Roger and I would consult about what I learned. The Internet and the phone were my tools and I used a list of questions for each agency I called. We also visited a social worker specializing in adoption, and she was the first person to mention China as a possibility. In mid-October 1999, we went to an information seminar by New Life Adoption Agency in Syracuse, NY, where we met a parent and her baby girl from China. Overall, we were impressed by the program and left feeling excited. Our baby would be in China, we felt sure of it.

THE REFERRAL

We were told that the wait would be six to nine months after our dossier went to China in May of 2000. It was not until March 29 of 2001, 10 months later, that we finally got the phone call from our agency. We had been checking the China adoption referral statistics website frequently to see how close we were getting and it seemed like it took forever for the May "DTC" (dossier to China) group to start getting the good news. The couple of weeks just before we got our phone call were excruciating—May DTCs were getting referrals and we were still waiting. It was a short phone call but it changed our lives immediately. We learned her Chinese name, Ji Cai Gen, and that she had been born one month after our paperwork landed in China, on June 11, 2000. Ji Cai Gen was in the Hua Zhou Children's Welfare Institute, about 200 miles south of Guangzhou. A Chinese friend interpreted her name for us as "Lucky Vegetable Root" but we later found out that the Chinese characters actually mean "Lucky Colorful Root." Either way we felt it was a good name and that it meant she would be happy and "down to earth."

The music of rustling pines.
The tinkling of spring water over rocks.
Everything entering your ears is part of Nature's chimes.
The haze over tall grasses.

The cloud's shadow amidst water.
Watching them at leisure is like reading the best essay of the
Universe.

—*Caigentan: The Zen of the Vegetable Root* by
Hong Ying Ming, Chinese scholar in Ming dynasty

The reality of the referral brought with it an increased level of excitement, and a bit of anxiety. She was real! She was waiting for us! Her medical report indicated that she was in good health, but we still knew we wouldn't rest easy until we had her in our arms. She was beautiful. . . .

We picked a new name for the baby soon after getting the referral. We had decided early on that we would keep her Chinese name for her middle name and we thought that "Cai Gen" was delightful. We agreed on Grace for her first name. It is my middle name and a family name that we both like very much. In my heart, Grace fit perfectly because this baby was indeed our gift from God. We kept Grace Cai Gen's name a secret from everyone until the day we left for China.

THE TRIP

One of the blessings of our trip to China was the group of other couples with whom we traveled. We met for the first time at a travel meeting a few weeks before the trip, five couples and one single Mom in all. . . . Because most of us were living in central NY at the time, four couples of our group flew out of Syracuse together, and we met the rest in San Francisco before the long flight over to Hong Kong. The intensity of the shared experience of traveling to meet our babies plus the trials of the long flight bonded us all into an extended family by the time we arrived in China. . . .

I couldn't sleep at all on the long flight over. I just couldn't bring myself to eat dinner when my body wanted breakfast, and the excitement of knowing we'd meet our daughter soon was stronger than coffee for keeping me awake. Babies were crying from time to time on the plane, and all I could think was "that will be us on the way home in a couple of weeks." The lack of sleep, jet lag, and excitement combined to create a surreal feeling by the time we were on the last little hop over from Hong Kong to Guangzhou. We could see lots of water and some beautiful mountainous islands as we took off, and the sky was clear blue, serene and peaceful, as we flew.

We had been told the babies would be brought to us at the hotel the same day we arrived. We were exhausted, hungry and in desperate need of a shower, but we were so close now that when our liaison, Frank, asked us if we wanted to eat lunch we replied in unison "No! Hotel!" Not enough wonderful things can be said about Frank. After collecting us like so many baby ducks and assessing our survival of the long trip (everyone fared fine and only one bag was lost, and luckily not one containing diapers or formula!), he herded us onto the air-conditioned bus and got us checked into the hotel rooms. That image of Frank gathering, herding, instructing, and sometimes gently scolding us like a group of ducklings came to me time and time again as he led us through the adoption and visa paper proceedings over the next ten days. He told us his previous careers included being a policeman and a teacher, and I can't think of better qualifications for his work with us nervous adoptive parents.

THE GIRLS

It was May 15, early afternoon in Guangzhou when we arrived. We had lost May 14th in flight. We were in our room only 5 minutes, still trying to figure out how to turn the lights on, when the phone rang. It was Frank. We were to meet in his room in 15 minutes—the babies were on their way! We took the fastest showers, quickly changed into fresh clothes, and hurried downstairs.

Frank's room was full of very excited people as we waited for the girls to arrive. Frank talked to us about the orphanage and other things to keep our minds occupied. We kept imagining we heard babies! About 3 P.M., finally the big moment arrived. The orphanage nannies came in with the six babies; all of us were trying to figure out who was who. Grace was turned away from us when she was first brought into the room, but when we finally caught sight of her we recognized her. When Grace's nanny brought her to us it was the most intense and wonderful moment of our lives. The tears rolled (ours, not hers). She came to us beautiful and quiet as a mouse, looking around with those big eyes. We took her back to our room to get acquainted, and make our first parental act of feeding her a bottle. She still did not make a peep (that would come later) and we found ourselves speaking softly, almost whispering, to her.

A little while later we met her nanny and the orphanage Assistant Director again, and learned a bit more about her routine and habits. Her nanny showed us how Grace could already walk if you held her two hands and told us that Grace was mischievous. Grace clearly was the most active baby in our group, pulling herself to a stand while holding on to furniture, although she wasn't really quite ready to walk (however she was walking on her own about a month and a half later). As for being mischievous, we interpreted this to mean that she was creative in finding ways to get attention in the orphanage, which no doubt served her well. . . .

The next day, May 16, we officially adopted Grace Cai Gen Landry. We were dream walking partly due to lack of sleep. Never could I imagine doing so much important new stuff without sleep for so long. The formal adoption interview and process went smoothly. My most poignant memory of the event was promising that yes, we would love this baby, and no, we would never abandon her. She was now our daughter.

SIGHTSEEING, DOCTORS, AND VISAS

Grace clung to us mostly silently for the first couple of days but as she adjusted to us she quickly came out of her shell. Grace was a good teacher and we learned her favorite baby games, like peek-a-boo in the mirror, and "flying baby." We were charmed by the way she greeted us with little head-bumps. While we waited for the paperwork to catch up with us we did some sightseeing around Guangzhou. The weather was dreadfully hot and humid, but off we went with babies in their snuglies, all of us sweating like crazy as we toured the city.

We visited the Buddhist temple of the six Banyan trees, the tomb of the Nanyue Emperor, and the Dr. Sun Yatsen Memorial Hall. My favorite excursion was to the park. . . . There were many families and children there and the entertainment included paddleboat rides and outdoor Chinese opera, badminton, ping-pong, pool, and many other games. The park itself was absolutely beautiful, impeccably maintained. Many people came up and asked us questions in Chinese and we learned that mostly they were asking us the age and gender of the babies. While we must have been quite a sight, the people in that part of the city were probably familiar with seeing adoptive families traipsing through the park. The people we met were curious and supportive; we got several "thumbs up" signs as we walked.

My least favorite trip was to the city hospital. Grace developed a rash on her head and limbs that had her constantly scratching, and she also had several sores that we were concerned about. . . . The hospital was excellent, immaculately clean, and apparently modern. The doctor who examined Grace was very professional and patient with us. . . . Grace had infected bug bites and a throat infection, which we treated with antibiotics and a lotion that looked like Calamine. . . . [She] kept right on scratching through the whole trip. In addition to the rash, we think it was just her way of dealing with all the sudden changes in her life.

As we approached the end of our stay we had to jump the final hurdle of getting the girls' American visas. The first phase of getting the visa was to have Grace's photo taken and get the medical check up. We had had a rough night with little sleep, so we weren't off to a good start that morning. We rode over to the White Swan hotel, which is near the American Consulate in a pretty part of the city by the Pearl River. There was a flood of families waiting with their babies to have passport photos taken, and here we realized again how fortunate we were to be a small group, and to have Frank. There was a lot of confusion in the crowd as we waited, and once inside we had to get the babies to sit just right so a photo could be taken that showed their ear. Grace's first take didn't work out, but miraculously we were able to get right back in and have a second photo done. Next, we literally ran, as a group, over to the clinic to get in line for the medicals. We wanted to get as early a start as possible before the crowds got even larger. Grace was not happy with the medical examination, in part because she was exhausted, as were we, and also because she did not like being undressed and dressed under any circumstances. . . . But, all went well and we were ready for the next step—the interview with the American Consulate.

Waiting for the interview was the most nerve-wracking part of the process. This was where all of our paperwork would be examined carefully and if, somehow, we had made any mistakes we would face uncertain consequences and would probably face delays for going home. It was important to be considerate and respectful in the tiny crowded waiting area because there were many families waiting and the officials needed to keep it quiet for the interviews, which took place in the same room. Needless to say, it was difficult with wiggly little babies. Even Frank seemed nervous for us; we held our breaths.

Our paperwork was OK and the interview was a breeze, a short conversation with the woman who examined our paperwork. One more quick trip the next day to pick up the visa and "Hooray!" Grace was ours in the eyes of the American government. Now we really felt like celebrating. Back at the White Swan we bought little souvenirs for Grace, including a silver "Happy Baby" bracelet, which we hoped might also work as a "Sleepy Baby" bracelet—we were all ready for some solid sleep.

HOMEWARD BOUND

Our final day in China was so hot that we decided to skip the trip to the zoo and stay in the room to rest and pack. I couldn't wait to pack! . . . It was the end of an intense and wonderful trip, the most wonderful of our lives. And it was time to go home.

At the Syracuse airport we were greeted by excited grandparents, family, and friends, as well as the local news station crew who captured the homecoming on tape. All of Grace's new grandparents, plus her Aunt Shelley and cousins Adam and Kendra were there to welcome her. Grace did admirably in all the commotion and what must have been overwhelming new sights, sounds and smells. We were exhausted from the trip and thankful to be home safe and sound with our new daughter. . . .

TODAY

Grace is now 26 months old and thriving. She is a happy, bright, playful little girl and the joy she brings to our lives can't be put into words. . . . She's a busy, curious toddler now, and she still excels at physical activities, running, jumping and climbing.

Adopting Grace has been far and away the best thing Roger and I have ever done. Creating a family by reaching halfway around the earth is a miracle. We are now connected to another country, another culture, in the most intimate of ways. As Grace grows we will all learn more about her Chinese heritage together, and we are pleased to have the friendship and support of other adoptive families and our Chinese American friends as we do.

A Gay Couple's Motives for Adoption

by Dan Savage

Dan Savage is a syndicated columnist and associate editor for the *Stranger*, an alternative weekly newspaper published in Seattle, Washington. He and his partner, Terry, are a gay couple that were eager to explore the possibility of raising a child. Savage initially sought a lesbian who would be willing to become a surrogate mother and co-parent a child, but after a few meetings with different women, none was willing to carry the plan through. This left Dan and Terry with only one alternative: adoption.

In the following excerpt from his book on the adoption experience, Savage discusses the reasons why he and his partner felt the desire to be parents. Children, he says, lessen parents' sense of mortality and give them a feeling of self-fulfillment. But as a gay man, Savage also recognizes that adopting a child is a political act since it runs contrary to the norms of a predominantly heterosexual society. Savage claims that he and his partner have to dwell on these motives since they will likely be called into question not only by an adoption agency but also by society at large.

Ultimately, Dan and Terry were able to adopt a baby boy through an open adoption process. In this case, the boy, D.J., will maintain an open and active relationship with his birth mother in order to lessen confusion about parental roles in the child's life. Savage and his partner were pleased with the agreement, and at the time the book went to print, they were already considering adopting a playmate for D.J.

There's a question I've been dodging. Why were we having a kid? Or kids, plural, I should say, because Terry and I . . . believed children should have siblings to torment. So, why kids? We were HIV-negative gay men living in America at the end of the twentieth century. Barring some social or economic disaster . . . , we had a long, prosperous DINK future spread out before us. (That's "Double Income, No Kids," our by-default consumer demographic.) Remaining DINKs meant a future of travel, parties, cheap-if-not-meaningless sex, health clubs, and swank homes. Why would any gay man in his right mind trade DINKdom for dirty diapers?

"The middle age of buggers is not to be contemplated without horror" [novelist] Virginia Woolf is reported to have observed. I don't believe there's anything horrid about middle-aged gay men (provided they don't join men's choruses or the North American Man-Boy Love Association, watch *Deep Space Nine*, or display teddy bears in little leather harnesses in their living rooms). Nevertheless, at about age thirty, I began to contemplate my impending middle age with a degree of horror. What was I going to *do* for the next forty or fifty years? It didn't take me long to conclude I would need more in my life than money and men. I would want something meaningful to do with my free time, something besides traveling the world collecting Fiesta Ware and intestinal parasites.

So, kids.

WHY HAVE A KID

Once upon a time, people had kids out of a sense of obligation to family, species, and society; and since they lacked birth control, most sexually active folks weren't in much of a position to prevent themselves from making babies. We've got birth control now, at least in most places, and we've got access to abortion, at least for now. While some couples feel pressured by their families or churches to have kids, for a large number of people in a large part of the world, having children is optional for the first time in history. Why do people have kids today? It's not to do the species a favor: the largest threat to our survival is our out-of-control breeding. The reason people in general (by which I mean straight people, since people in general are straight) have kids today is to give themselves something real and meaningful and important to do. Having children is no longer about propagating the species or having someone to leave your lands to, but about self-fulfillment. Kids are a self-actualization project for the parents involved. . . . Something for grownups to do, a pastime, a hobby.

So why not kids? Gay men need hobbies, too.

Our other options as gay men at the end of the twentieth century—how to occupy our time over the next thirty years—were not at all appealing. Terry and I had, basically, three choices:

Option 1: Stay in the Game. Keep going to bars, and parties, and clubs, keep getting laid, keep drinking, keep taking drugs. This option leads, inevitably, to our breakup over some humpy young thing, who would in turn dump us for a humpier younger thing. Eventually we become a couple of fifty-year-old fags hanging out in gay bars full of men too young to care that we, you know, Marched on Washington in '93. To compete with and compete for the annual crop of just-out twenty-one-year-old gay boys, we have to go under the knife again and again, until we are so much scar tissue stitched to scar tissue. Then we die. Our corpses, drug- and silicone-contaminated superfund sites, are denied a decent burial. Distant relatives come to town, crate us up, and haul us to a toxic-waste incinerator.

Option 2: Go Places, See Sh——. We stay together and spend our DINK dollars traveling the world. We take a lot of pictures, collect a lot of junk, have a lot of sex with the locals. Provided we don't succumb to Alzheimer's or some as-yet-undiscovered sexually transmitted disease, we have our memories to keep us company when we're old and gray. Then we die, our memories dying with us. Distant relatives come to town and haul us and everything else—photo albums, postcard collection, STD meds—off to the dump.

Option 3: Mr. & Mr. Martha Stewart. We buy a house and direct the passion we used to devote to sex to the renovation and decoration of our little manse. We spend the last years of our lives combing junque stores, yard sales, estate sales, and auction houses for that authentic Victorian/Edwardian/Art Deco/Fab Fifties nightstand/hall table/mirror/dinette set that will finally complete our beautiful-but-sterile home. Once we find it, our local newspaper's Sunday magazine does a photo spread of our to-die-for home. Then we die. Distant relatives come to town, sell the house and the furniture, and donate our ancient bodies to science.

KIDS KEEP MORTALITY AT BAY

I was already planning on having kids when I met Terry, so I'd already thought through all of this. After I walked Terry through what I saw as our options, he agreed that they were pretty depressing. Each ended with distant relatives coming to town and disposing of our remains in a tremendously unsentimental manner. And everything we would have DINKed so hard for—our possessions, our memories, our hair systems—would be busted up and thrown away.

Mortality is unsettling, and the more we thought about having kids the more sense they made as hedges against depressing, lonely deaths. We didn't want to be anybody's forgotten old gay uncles.

Kids wouldn't keep us young, but they would keep us relevant, something other hobbies wouldn't do. If we had kids and they managed to outlive us, Terry and I would be hauled off to the dump when our time came by people who knew us and felt obligated to dispose of us.

So, kids.

Yes, I know: kids die, kids turn out rotten, kids grow up to be serial killers, kids abandon their parents, kids *kill* their parents. Adopted kids may decide their biological relatives are their *real* relatives and blow off their adoptive families. Kids are a crap-shoot. But even if the only thing your kids give a sh— about is getting their hands on your money or your Holden-Wakefield end tables, even if all your kids want is for you to drop dead, at least someone is giving a specific sort of sh— about you. And if you have more than one kid who wants your end tables, you can have fun drafting and redrafting your will.

Sometimes, late at night, I'd sit up and worry that we might be adopting to prove a point. Were we doing this because we could? On some level, I think, we were. It wasn't the sole reason, but even if we were only doing this to prove something to the world or to ourselves, there are worse reasons to have kids. Straight people all over the world have kids for those much worse reasons every day. They fall down drunk and get up pregnant.

The same impulse that drives grown gay men to walk around holding hands could be pushing us toward this. For same-sex couples, taking a lover's hand is almost never an unself-conscious choice. You have to think about where you are, whether you're safe, and you have to look. By the time you determine you're safe, you're not even sure you want to hold hands anymore. The genuine moment has passed, but you've invested so much energy and angst that now you can't *not* take your lover's hand. You wind up holding and the only reason you take your lover's hand is to prove that you can.

Wondering whether we were doing this "just to prove we can," made us wonder about our motives. In that hesitation, the decision to adopt became more than "Let's have kids." Public displays of affection for gays and lesbians are political acts, and what could be a larger public display of affection than the two of us adopting a kid together.

Taking Over as the Mother of My Brother-in-Law's Children

by Nancy Hanner

In 1992 Nancy Hanner and her husband became the adoptive parents of her niece and nephew when her husband's sister and brother-in-law died in separate incidents. In the following narrative, Hanner, a resident of Lexington, Kentucky, tells of how taking on the responsibility for raising two young children has been a confusing and trying experience. Gaining two youngsters overnight altered Hanner's plans for starting a family of her own, and she initially wondered if raising children who were not her own would complicate their mother/child relationship. Over time, though, Hanner came to realize that she should not overanalyze the complexities of her situation and instead acknowledge that providing a loving family atmosphere is the best thing she can do for her adopted children.

E leven years ago [in 1992], I arrived at the funeral of my brother-in-law as both a mourning relative and the sudden legal guardian of his two children. It was the family's second funeral in the course of a year. Nine months earlier, my sister-in-law, niece and nephew had died in a tragic accident. People approached me, pressed my hands and said, "You are so wonderful to take these children."

It was a noble view of adoption, with me the rescuer, the saver of children. It was tempting to buy into it, and I did at times. But once I got down to the business of raising children, I found that that perspective had little to do with the reality of creating a family.

After the funeral, my husband and I moved into my brother-in-law's house so we wouldn't further disrupt the lives of our new 18-month-old son and 2-year-old daughter. Those first three months were so stressful I developed a case of hives that I couldn't shake.

The hives eventually want away, but it took a lot longer to work through the emotional problems. Despite my best efforts at forging a relationship with her, my daughter gave me the cold shoulder for the first five years she was with us. Her favorite story was "Cinderella," and I'm fairly certain I wasn't the Fairy Godmother.

BEING NO. 2

I have a friend who became a full-time stepmother one weekend when her husband's ex-wife decided she could no longer care for the children. She raised the kids, monitoring late-night asthma attacks, baking room-mother treats and sitting through Scout meetings.

"My daughter invited me to the mother's weekend at college," she told me one day. "Then she found out her real mother could make it, so she called back to uninvite me."

I was shocked at her daughter's heartless treatment of the mother who had always been there for her. My friend and I are No. 2—we will never truly be No. 1 in our kids' eyes, and that is one of the not-so-nice realities of adoption.

We are quick to point out what we consider our children's misdirected loyalties, but what of our own? My friend's preference would have been to have raised a traditional family with her husband. Mine was also to have children of my own, which I attempted to do without success for seven years. However much we pretend otherwise, our adopted children were second choices for us.

So there it is. Our children want what they have lost, and so do we. They have lost their blood ties to parents. We have lost our visions of family, the dream of how our lives should look.

PURE LOVE OF A FAMILY

I recently read about a family who brought a baby girl back from China. The whole family passionately wanted to do this. The oldest son comes home from college more often now so he can play with her. The kids developed a schedule because they all wanted to hold her at the same time. This family adopted their daughter for the purest of reasons: they had love to give, and felt compelled to offer it. That's all. So many people don't start in the right place as this family did, but those who are willing to work through the disillusionment that follows have a chance to grow into a real family unit.

A few months ago my 12-year-old daughter called from her grandmother's house, where she was visiting for the week. She has a special bond with this grandmother, the mother of the mother she lost. "I miss the dog," she said, then laughed. "Oh, and I miss you, too." When I hung up, I was glad for all those years that we moved slowly together, circling each other—afraid to place our vulnerability in each other's hands. She did miss me. I could hear it in her voice.

My son is now old enough to understand chromosomes and the steps beyond the mechanics of reproduction. My husband's blood runs through my son, but mine does not, and he knows it. "There is a ceremony," I told him, thinking this would appeal greatly to an 11-year-old boy, "where we can become blood brothers. We can do it if you want." He considered it and said no, I imagine because of the part involving blood. Now I wonder if it was I who wanted the ceremony, if I was still longing for the solidity of a blood bond.

I feel ridiculous for having suggested this idea, realizing he has no need for such things—that he is, in fact, exactly where he should be. He knows where his family is, both the one that is buried and the one that sits at the hockey rink, watching him play. And because he is such a great kid, he is willing to be patient with a mother who sometimes likes to make her mission much more complicated than what it really is: the offering of family, simple, sweet and pure.

Adopting a Special-Needs Child

by Jean-Marie Wilson

Choosing to adopt a child is a major undertaking, but adopting a child with special needs requires a unique commitment that not all prospective parents are willing to make. In the following narrative, Jean-Marie Wilson explains what convinced her family to take in Joey, a five-year-old boy with physical deformities who was both undersized and underweight. As Wilson states, she and her husband fell in love with the boy and wanted to rescue him from an unwelcoming foster care environment. Ironically, though, once the Wilson family showed their commitment to Joey, Wilson claims that Joey's doctor and his school caretakers refused to believe that the adoption was for the boy's benefit. Wilson maintains, however, that under her and her husband's care, Joey has excelled physically and exceeded the limited expectations of all those who had previously doubted his capabilities.

When I was pregnant with my first child, I told my best friend that Steve [and] I would adopt some day. I even called the county social services department and asked about adoption. We were invited to an information meeting but never went. We both worked full-time. Eventually we had three children, all in daycare or private school. I knew we couldn't afford another child. Besides, our lives were too busy.

And then, Steve and I were both laid off from our jobs. We had to take the children out of private school and daycare. Slowly, over a period of two years, we pulled ourselves out of the bad times. We rearranged our lives and got used to lower-paying jobs and fewer luxuries. Our children stayed in public schools. We started seriously talking about adoption. I called the Department of Social Services. We were invited to an information meeting, and this time we went. Adopting through the county also required 18 hours of training classes, and we began these classes as soon as we could.

WAITING

Our children were 11, 9, and 7 at the time and didn't seem to mind our adding another child. They only wanted to know that we were not adopting due to some deficiency on their part. We assured them that we loved them, and that's why we wanted another child.

I used to take long walks on my lunch hour, praying we would be approved, and praying for the child who would be ours. I often wondered how people survived the waiting without God.

A week after we received our county license, our social worker left a message on our answering machine: "Watch Wednesday's Child on the news and call to let me know what you think." Steve was working, but all three children and I watched the program. I still have the piece of paper I took notes on, describing the little boy we saw. The children stayed up until Steve got home. He agreed to this child, without having seen him. Considering the child is physically challenged, this was an act of faith on Steve's part!

Steve and I spent the next six weeks battling the social workers. Our new son had spent most of his life in one foster home. His social worker wanted them to adopt him, but they refused. Social Services then wanted to change his status to a permanent foster child in their home. Considering the foster family moved out of state two years later, it is a good thing that arrangement never happened.

Finally, they brought his picture to us, along with his life book and a video of him. We saw a little boy with brown hair, brown eyes, and olive skin. He also had a shortened right arm with a "paddle" hand (no thumb, webbed partial fingers), a left hand with webbing and contractures, and he wore leg braces. Although he was almost six years old, he only weighed 25 pounds and was barely three feet tall.

BRINGING JOEY HOME

We met Joey two months after we saw him on television. Over the next few weeks, he spent evenings with us. I picked him up at his foster home on my way home from work, and took him back in time for bed. We started moving his things in, and he spent a weekend with us. I was having a hard time finding daycare for him (this was before the Americans with Disabilities Act). He was also getting to bed late because I honestly hated giving him back. His foster mother offered to provide daycare, so he could move in with us, while giving him time to (mentally) transition to our home. I eventually found a daycare center and got his special education bus changed, and Joey was ours and in our home.

Because his foster mother had Joey for so long, we met resistance at school (he stayed in the same school). After all, we had "taken" him from his mother. His doctor told us we didn't understand his condition, and we shouldn't have adopted him. It took almost two years for them to realize we loved him and cared about him!

Joey was "helpless" when he came to us. There were some things he pretended he could not do, such as putting on his shirt, and some things he really could not do, such as self-toilet. He also told me his teachers took his lunch from him, not letting him finish eating. Actually, he ate slowly, and often didn't have time to finish his lunch. He also seemed to throw up a lot. I quickly learned that behavior was a bid for attention—and a day off school. That stopped when I made him stay in bed all day whenever he was "sick," instead of letting him lie on the couch and watch television.

Joey hated to chew food and was in the habit of stuffing his cheeks with food and letting his saliva break it down. After constantly reminding him to chew, we've almost broken that habit. He grew and started gaining weight.

He would complain that his leg braces hurt, especially when we were out in public or in the car. It took me two or three years to figure out that he could wear them all day if they were made properly. A switch to a different orthotist made the difference. By the end of Joey's first year with us, he could self-toilet, dress/undress himself, including his braces, and bathe himself. In other words, he could do everything for himself.

We were named Montgomery County (Maryland) Adoptive Family of the Year in 1991. A reporter asked the adoption supervisor why we were chosen as Joey's parents. She admitted to asking us to watch the television program so we "could see what type of child" they had available. They didn't "pick" us for Joey. It was over six weeks of nagging that got him placed with us.

I started attending adoption conferences. After one particularly wonderful workshop, I called our HMO's mental health facility. After testing and counseling, a four-year suspicion of mine was confirmed. Joey is ADD [i.e., has attention deficit disorder]. He's now on medication, and it helps him quite a bit. Joey still has problems. He continues to pretend to be helpless with every new teacher and then wonders why they get so mad at him when they realize he's faking. He still swears he doesn't have any homework when, in fact, he does. He's still about ⅔ the height and half the weight of children his age.

WE LOVE HIM

He initially had contact with his birth mother, through the social worker. She stopped writing and sending gifts a year or two ago.

Joey has been with us over six years, and we love him. At first our other children were worried about how they'd adapt to a brother who is physically challenged. Now they don't even think about it. Joey has friends his age and friends through his brother and sisters. It seems that everywhere we go, someone knows Joey.

In addition, Joey is an excellent writer. So far he has been published twice, and he has entered one writing contest. He's currently working on a mystery story.

Joey has had problems dealing with the usual grief issues all adopted children deal with. I've been lucky in finding him counseling through an adoption agency. I have found that most therapists are not familiar with adoption issues and the behaviors of children adopted out of foster care.

Our families have accepted Joey and take real pleasure in spending time with him. Joey still has difficulty spending the night at a friend's house—he goes into his "helpless act." He also has difficulty with my husband and I going away for a weekend. He still needs to be reassured that someone will always be there to take care of him.

Love never fails. (1 Corinthians 13:8)

CHAPTER 3

Adoptee Experiences

How I Learned That I Was Adopted

by B.G. Blackburn

In the following narrative, a woman referring to herself as B.G. ("baby girl") Blackburn discusses what she calls "bastard moments"—instances in her life when her family made her feel like a black sheep or an illegitimate child. Blackburn says that she initially didn't think too deeply about them; however, once she discovered that she had been adopted, such moments assumed a new, deeper significance.

Perhaps the most telling bastard moment that Blackburn recounts involves her stepmother, the second wife of her adoptive father. As Blackburn explains, her stepmother would introduce her to visitors as a friend of the family's eldest daughter, not as a stepdaughter. While it seemed a bit odd, Blackburn says that she thought little of it until her adoptive father failed to introduce her as his daughter on a separate occasion. Blackburn marks this as the moment when she figured out that she was adopted. After discerning the truth, Blackburn says that her adoptive father made a halfhearted attempt to explain everything to her, but by that point his words were little consolation.

Blackburn attributes the behavior of her family to their lack of ability to live with the shame of her illegitimacy. While she is not happy about the way things unfolded, Blackburn maintains that she draws a sense of identity from being a bastard child.

In her book, *Journey of the Adopted Self*, Betty Jean Lifton coins the term "bastard moments." I think of a bastard moment as a kind of Calgon Moment scripted by [suspense director Alfred] Hitchcock. You are in your warm, steamy, cozy bathroom, a tub full of warm water and scented suds awaits you. You dip in a toe, a foot, step in, pull in your other foot. Only then do you realize that what you thought was a bubble is actually a large, hairy spider swimming toward your leg, its closest shoreline. You jump out, slip on the tiles, and bang your head. You want to scrub yourself furiously, but the tub is already occupied by a horror.

I was almost 28 when I learned that I was adopted. Until then, I certainly thought I was the legitimate product of my parents' marriage (such as that marriage was—which was not much). Still, I had had bastard moments already, though I didn't know the term then.

GETTING TO KNOW DAD'S "OTHER FAMILY"

My parents, always emotionally estranged, split up for good when I was 12, though they didn't divorce until I was in my 20s. From then on, I saw my father occasionally. He would take me to dinner or out to a movie, or shopping. But I knew nothing of his personal life, that he had another family, and I never visited him in his home. There were good reasons for this; he and I both would have paid a huge price if my mother had known about that family. She was a vindictive woman.

But at 22, I was ready to know his family, I no longer worried about what my mother would think, and I would visit his home occasionally. I learned that I had a half-sister only 18 months younger than me. I had no trouble accepting this. My father and his wife were happy with one another, and who was I to judge when that happiness began? I was glad that he had a happy home life, something my mother could never have given him, or, for that matter, anyone around her.

My first bastard moment came when my stepmother, a truly nice woman, hesitantly told me that they had decided, for the time being, to introduce me as my half sister's friend, rather than as my father's daughter from his first marriage. Though my father and stepmother had never married (and haven't still, as far as I know), they had been living as a family for so long, and hiding the fact of his previous marriage for so long that none of their friends knew Dad had been married before, or that he had had other children.

Odd though it may seem, I was barely conscious at the time of any hurt. I thought it was ironic that his legitimate daughter was being treated as a secret, while his illegitimate daughter, my half-sister, was considered legitimate by everyone who knew him. I was anxious to please, and anxious to fit in with his immediate and extended family (none of whom I had met before, at least not after the age of three). What hurt I felt I buried in irony. Remember that I did not know that I was adopted then, and wouldn't for another six years.

A TRUE BASTARD MOMENT

And then came a true bastard moment, perhaps three years after these visits started. I was about 25. Dad and I were sitting at the kitchen table when a young third cousin of his dropped in unexpectedly. She was about my age, and looked so much like people in Dad's family. The three of us sat, I was introduced by name, but not by relationship to this cousin of mine. It was obvious from their talk that these visits were not unusual, that they kept up with one another's lives.

And then she turned to me and asked what nationality I was.

She didn't know. Three years I had been back in Dad's life, and although he knew that this cousin was in law school, and she knew about his health and retirement and all these other details, she did not know about me.

I was stunned, and all the hurt that I had not felt three years before at being introduced as an acquaintance came over me.

There was an awkward pause. My father and I stared at each other. Not a word was said, but the exchange between us was almost audible, at least to me. "I'm sorry." "How could you?" "Please." "How could you?"

"I only ask," she went on, "because I have a friend who looks like you, and she's Serbian."

"I'm the same as you," I replied, knowing how absurd it sounded. We look nothing alike. I turned to my father. "Want more coffee, Dad?"

The visit ended, nothing was said by anyone, then or later, and I never have seen that cousin again.

INFERRING THE TRUTH

My mother died when I was 27. I was out of the country. She hadn't been ill, and there was no reason to expect her to die while I was away for those four months. She died on Thanksgiving day, but I knew nothing about it until December 1, when I received a fax at the Central Telegraph office, sent by the State Department. It was my older sister, also adopted, who had decided the fax should be sent. Dad figured there was nothing I could do about it, so he would have waited till I returned to tell me.

Two months later, I was back in the States, sitting in a restaurant with my father and stepmother. Dad said, "There's something I have to tell you, something you should have been told when you were little. . . ." He talked for another 15 minutes or so, never coming to the point. Later, I learned that my stepmother had kicked him under the table, worried that I would burst into tears or have a breakdown in public. I have no idea what he said after those first sentences, because they were all I needed to understand. He finished up with, "I'll tell you the rest when we get home." Actually, he told me the rest at breakfast three days later. In the meantime, though, I thought he must mean that I was adopted, but I wasn't sure. I wondered if it were wishful thinking, a childish fantasy that had been given a boost by circumstances.

I remember the first night after his aborted speech at the restaurant, how I was lying in bed with my heart pounding, thinking that I had finally got what I wanted—maybe! Maybe I wasn't really related to that crazy woman who raised me and her crazy family. Maybe all of this nonsense, this secrecy, this goddamn dysfunction was not my burden, because I was not related to these people at all. Maybe that's why I don't look like them. Act like them. Share their tastes. That's why I have these interests that they don't, and unheard of preferences, dislikes, and talents.

Dad finished the story three days later, at breakfast, and that was *not*, most emphatically *not*, a bastard moment. It was liberation.

"I want to finish that story," he said.

"You don't need to. I've already guessed."

"It never made no difference to me."

"I know."

It was my mother's death that prompted the telling. Not because she had never wanted me to know (she hadn't), but because the lawyer handling the estate made it clear that I would find out, one way or another, so I had better find out in a decent way, rather than from some ratty legal document.

Later, we went to the family room and the file was pulled out and I read that for the first seven months of my life, I was Baby Girl Blackburn, and that I had had a different mother, and that my mother had a name. I sat on the couch and read. My heart pounded again, and the world fell away. I was dizzy with the knowledge. It changed everything. It explained so much.

My last bastard moment—or now, anyway—was a memory. The mother I grew up with had, not to put too fine a point on it, a mouth like a sailor. And when my sister and I would fight, or I would annoy her in some way, she would call me names. All sorts of names. But the one that sticks in my mind now, above all the others, is "You little bastard!" Even then, I thought it odd to call a girl that. I thought it was only for boys. I was wrong.

The irony of it. My birth was apparently so shameful that I had to be given away. The adoption that should have legitimized me was shameful, hidden by my parents and by the state. And as I grew up, I was bastardized again by my father and his family, to cover up their own unnecessary shame and perceived illegitimacy. A bastard I was born, and a bastard I remain. Lies and shame made it so.

Forgiving My Adoptive Mother for Not Telling Me

by Ron Morgan

Ron Morgan is a "late discovery adoptee." That is, he did not realize that he was adopted until late in life. In fact, Morgan did not discover the truth of his origin until after his adoptive mother and father had passed away. In the following narrative, Morgan discusses his reaction to the revelation and how he dealt with the emotions that came as a result.

Attempting to put his confusion and grief out of his mind, Morgan spent years coping with the issue of his adoption. However, Morgan found it difficult to settle his temper in the absence of his adoptive mother. As Morgan explains, it took an extraordinary act for him to forgive his adoptive mother for not telling him that he was adopted.

Ron Morgan is very active in adoption support groups, including serving as the Event's Chairman for Bastard Nation, one such organization. He also writes and gives lectures on the effects of late discovery adoption.

T his Mother's Day will come, and after my kids give Loren their homemade cards, and after I have some coffee and a half dozen morning cigarettes, I will hike up Bernal Mountain to visit my a-mom.

Bernal Mountain isn't much of a mountain, just an undeveloped promontory above my neighborhood, bristling with microwave antennas, laced with trails and dog runs. There are a couple of rock croppings that jut out toward the city skyline, and there is where I will sit. From these rocks I spread my mother's ashes, June 18, 1995.

I don't have much to say to her. The words have all been spewed out of me, during visits to the beach in the dead of night, with letters asking, "Why?" and longer entreaties, which I offered up to her memory in a blazing Bic sacrifice, hoping the smoke might catch her

Ron Morgan, "Mother's Day," *Bastard Quarterly*, Summer 1997. Copyright © 1997 by Ron Morgan. Reproduced by permission.

attention. When that didn't seem to work, I'd yell at the surf. And go home. And look at the box containing her ashes.

THE SPECTER OF CARMEN

The box arrived one day while I was at work. The UPS man remarked that the parcel seemed heavy for one so small. Loren said, "Of course its heavy, it's my mother-in-law." The Neptune Society had f—ed up and sent it to me, against the instruction and payment to store her until I figured out what to do with her. Interring her next to my father was prohibitively expensive, as he was buried cheek to jowl with some army buddies, and would have to be moved to a new spot along with Carmen. That was her name, Carmen. I couldn't figure out what to do with her. I was torn between chucking her out of a moving car and fevered grandiose gestures of memorial storage. The only thing I knew for sure was she didn't want to be scattered into the ocean, because she told me so several times over a course of 30 years.

She left no specific instructions, though, so I put her on a shelf beneath the shrine I used to meditate. Instead of insight meditation, I did this: Breathe in: my mother sitting at her dressing table, telling me the stories of her family, chatting, turning, and wiping a smudge from my face with a Kleenex dampened by her spit. Breathe out: why did you lie to me? How could you lie to me? Why did you lie to me? Repeat.

I stopped meditating. I put Carmen in a drawer. I discussed my dilemma with Loren, but no one else. Carmen shamed me from the drawer, then from a shelf where I used her for a bookend, then back to the shrine, because though I didn't have a clue what I was doing, I did know that as an ex-person she deserved some sort of sacred space, however provisional that may have been.

DEALING WITH THE TRUTH

Discovering I was adopted a couple of weeks after Carmen's death put a big crimp in my grieving cha-cha. Every mournful memory was woven into a curse. I eventually succeeded in not thinking about it for long stretches of time, but that didn't make it any better when I did. Years passed, and I let this reproachful situation eat at me slowly.

Then something clicked, I don't know what, maybe nothing more than the same urge that gets us out of an uncomfortable chair we've been sitting in too long. I chose her birthday, and after dinner I went to the basement to prepare her. She was in an embossed metal box, welded shut for an apparent eternity, and I had to use an old fashioned can opener to cut it open. It was a struggle. I worried about letting fly her ashes to the basement floor, commingling with redwood sawdust and bits of solder droppings. She was placidly resting in an ultra heavy duty plastic bag, tied at the top with a twistie.

I strode up the hill with Carmen's baggy nested within a double Safeway [grocery store] plastic shopping bag under one arm, disguised because I had become aware that what I planned was illegal, and counting prayer beads with the other hand, because I was praying a Buddhist rosary as I went. I was undisturbed as I stood on the rock outcropping watching the city radiating out from the foot of Bernal Mountain. I searched the night sky for the owl that lives up there, but she was out, hunting. I talked to Carmen, look I'm still f—ing mad as hell, but I can't keep this up. Rest here, I like this place, I come here a lot. I hope you're happy (this last said in earnest).

I opened the twistie and threw the baggy up, holding the bottom corners. Instead of the even, gentle dispersal I had imagined, my mother's ashes came out in three or four heavy lumps, and formed some odd but distinct shapes on the ground a few feet away. I crawled down and spread her around a bit.

Then I left. It rained lightly two days later, and washed the hill.

An Asian Adoptee Struggles to Fit In

by Tanawan Free

Seventeen-year-old Tanawan Free wrote the following narrative in response to being asked what it is like to be adopted. Free, who was adopted from Thailand and brought to the United States when he was two years old, says that being adopted initially meant recognizing how different he was from those around him. Free does not look like his adoptive family, and he is one of the few people of Asian descent in his predominantly Caucasian community. Because of these differences, Free struggled with not seeming to fit in with his new life for many years. When he reached high school, however, Free came to realize that everyone was different in his or her own way, and that these differences made each person unique. Since this revelation, Free has come to accept being adopted as just another part of who he is.

"What is it like to be adopted?" I was adopted when I was two and a half years old from Bangkok, Thailand, and brought to the states. I am now almost 18 years old. I have grown up in a small suburban city, where most of the people around are Caucasian. I am Asian, making me different from many of the people that live near me. Recognizing that I am adopted is something that has brought up many feelings, good and bad, which I would like to share with you. Firstly, adoption is a natural part of my life, secondly, I do not look like my parents, and lastly, I believe that everyone must come to an acceptance of being adopted in their own way and time.

Being adopted is something that is an unchangeable fact of my life, just as I have black hair and brown eyes. Being adopted is something that I have been exposed to all of my life. I have a full family of six, including me and three sisters who are all adopted. My parents founded an adoption agency and are in support of adoption in all that they do. My parents have taken my sisters and me to the countries that we come from; to let us learn about the country where we were born. Being adopted has become part of me. It is something that I cannot change or let go of, whether I want to, or not. There is one part of being adopted that I struggled with, which is that my parents look nothing like me.

EVERYONE WANTS TO BELONG

My parents are Caucasian, and I am Asian, with dark skin. Being different than my parents brought up some identity issues, like "who am I?" and "why am I the only one that is this way?" Looking different is the one thing that is more obvious than that of any other trait, and in middle school, being different was not cool, and I felt not cool because of it. I felt like I was the only one in the world that was adopted, blinding myself to the fact that my own sisters and cousins are adopted. Everyone wants to belong to something, and I wanted to belong somewhere, but it seemed like I was all by myself for a while. I was struggling with not feeling like I fit in anywhere, so I began to make up new, false identities to fit in where I could. I did many things to block out any difference that appeared. It took up until high school to start to accept being adopted was ok.

By the time that I had gotten to high school, my parents had tried to help me as much as they possibly could, but accepting the fact that I was adopted became my own struggle. It took me a long time to realize that it was acceptable to be different and that I was not the only adopted person in the world. During high school, I looked around and saw that everyone was different in some way, and it was ok. In high school, everyone wants to be different and stand out in some odd way, and for once, my difference seemed ok. Finally, I have grown to accept that being adopted is just a different way of life, and being different is something that is good.

Being adopted is something that I have grown to accept. It took me a few years, even with a family that was open to adoption in nearly every possible way. It took my feeling ok with it for me to be open about adoption as well. Now adoption is a fact of my life that I am able to talk about openly with people. I credit my parents for being able to talk with me about it and being willing to work with me. I can look back and see how much I had to struggle, but once I accepted that it was ok, I was able to be myself.

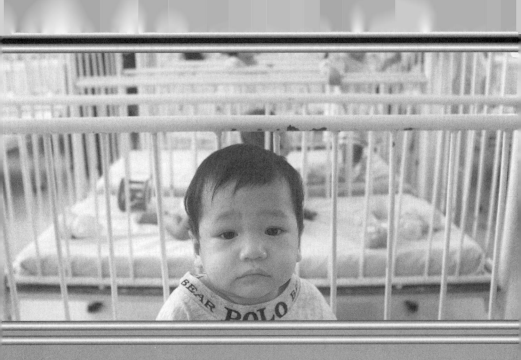

Searching for and Reuniting
with Birth Mothers

The Lengthy Searching Process

by Angry Grandma

The following narrative was written by a woman who uses the pseudonym "Angry Grandma" to express her anger at the treatment of women in American society. Specifically, she believes that many women have been forced to give up their children to adoption unnecessarily, resulting in suffering for both birth mothers and adoptees. Angry Grandma was adopted in 1953 from the St. Peter's Children's Home, an orphanage located in Memphis, Tennessee. In her narrative Angry Grandma explains the laborious search she undertook late in life in order to find her birth mother, Mary.

Angry Grandma gives an account of the numberless hours spent going over birth records, reading obituaries, writing letters, and making phone calls. According to her, if she came upon a lead, she would feel compelled to thoroughly follow it up. She even went as far as to hire professional investigators to help her in her search. It was, in fact, through one investigator that Angry Grandma was able to locate her birth mother.

In an interesting twist of fate, Angry Grandma also learned through her searches that her mother had given up another daughter to adoption. Pulling the various strands together, Angry Grandma was eventually able to reap the fruits of her extensive searching and reunite with her mother and her long-lost sibling.

I searched for my birthmother, Mary, for two years. When I began searching, I knew only my birthname, my brother's birthname, and the year and place of our adoption. This is a considerable amount of information for an adoptee beginning a search, and I feel fortunate to have known so much—many searching adoptees begin with no information other than their own birthdates, and we often aren't sure of the accuracy of that basic bit of information.

I have been blessed by the help of several individuals who volunteered at different stages of this search. Without the help of these internet angels, I would not have found my birthmother and sister. There are many wonderful people who gave support and search assistance along the way. . . .

GATHERING INFORMATION AND FOLLOWING LEADS

By June 1996, a wealth of information had been gathered about Mary. I knew her full name, her birth date, her parents' names, her grandparents' names, her family's address when she was born, the address she used when I was born, the names of her brother and sister, and even the name of one of her nephews. I knew where she had probably gone to elementary and junior high school. I knew where and when she and my father had been married, and that they both had been married previously. I knew when, where and why they had been divorced, the witnesses who testified at the divorce hearing, and why my mother had lost my brother and me to adoption. I knew when Mary's father had died, where he was buried, and the names of his survivors. I knew the full names of 110 women named Mary in the United States with the same birth date as my birthmother. I had spoken personally with several dozen women who were NOT "my" Mary, but who might have been, and had called scores of individuals in an attempt to find Mary or any of her living relatives.

I had obtained my non-identifying information, copies of my parents' marriage license and divorce papers, my baptism certificate, and the obituaries of people I ultimately found were NOT related to Mary, but who might have been. I subscribed to the Adoptees Mailing List and a genealogy news group, spent hundreds of hours browsing, locating and registering with every online registry I could find. . . .

I put web pages up on the internet, listing my birth name and all the information I knew about Mary. I listed myself by birth name in every searchable database I could find. I e-mailed and called dozens of Carrolls, Delanceys, Sergersons, and DuBois families across the U.S. I called newspapers, libraries, courthouses, county clerks, funeral homes and cemeteries. I wrote numerous letters to Social Security and obtained a dozen Social Security applications for women named Mary who had died, and made all the calls necessary to determine conclusively that they were not my Mary. I had been told by one paid searcher and by the Social Security Administration (most recently in June 1996) that Mary was dead. Every false report of her death had to be investigated.

Despite the hundreds of calls, letters, e-mails, postings, and the database of information accumulated, I had located only one person who had ever known Mary—my paternal uncle, who had not seen her since the early '50's, and had not known she'd placed her children for adoption.

A Social Security death index search revealed that my birthfather had died in 1991. His surviving brother was located, and we began communicating through telephone calls in 1995. My uncle told me he had several photograph albums of pictures, that he knew he had pictures of my father, and thought he might have pictures of my mother. Of course, I wanted to see those photographs of my birthparents, and to meet Uncle Eddie, my only known living "before me" blood relative.

For our 10th wedding anniversary present to each other, my husband and I planned a trip for June 1996, to meet Uncle Eddie. We purchased our airline tickets and made all our travel plans in March 1996. I planned to continue the search for Mary in Nashville, her birthplace. I researched the available information remaining to be reviewed, contacted the Tennessee State Library and determined the information available in their archives, as well as that available only through a review of individual county records (such as marriage licenses). In May 1996, faced with the overwhelming hours of research still remaining, and the very real possibility that we would still fail to locate Mary or anyone who knew her, my (incredibly patient and understanding) husband and I decided to hire a private investigator in Memphis, where Mary was last known to have lived in 1953, to continue the search. Realistically, we knew there was a very real possibility that the investigator would fail to locate any information about Mary, or worse, would find that she had died. We felt we would be lucky to find even one living relative of Mary's, but knew that a professional "on the ground" where Mary had lived was our best hope. We hired Nate Lenow on May 11, 1996.

HITTING PAY DIRT

On May 17, Nate told me that he had discovered, by looking in her divorce file, the name of Mary's employer at the time of her 1953 divorce. The company was still in business and he had contacted the personnel manager, who informed him that someone else had called within the previous few months, looking for Mary. Nate initially assumed this had been a "bogus" call made by me or for me in an attempt to locate Mary—but I assured him that Mary's former employer's name was new information for me, and that no one I knew had made that call.

I waited two weeks on pins and needles to hear who had contacted Mary's former employer, and on May 30 again contacted Nate by e-mail asking for a progress report.

His e-mail reply: "I have you scheduled for a miracle before you leave for Nashville." I printed this extraordinary message and taped it to my computer at work, where I would glance at it throughout the day, thinking, "That's all I ask." On June 18, eight days before my husband and I were scheduled to fly to Nashville, the miracle began unfolding.

AN UNEXPECTED DISCOVERY

On June 18, Nate called my office. He said, "The person looking for your mother is her daughter." I couldn't grasp what he was saying.

"Your sister," he said.

"I have a sister?"

"Yes, her name is Carol."

I had a sister, two years younger than me—born to Mary while she was still married to my birthfather—before I had been placed for adoption—a possibility I had never considered. I was stunned by this news and I wandered through my office telling everyone, "I just found out that I have a sister." "I have a sister!" That night Carol and I talked on the phone for the first time. She told me she'd known about me since she was 14 and had longed for her lost sister for years.

Importantly, Carol knew the name of the man Mary had married 40 years ago. On June 19, less than 24 hours after talking with my sister, I called Ron Layton [another professional investigator on the case] and gave him the name Carol had provided. He immediately recognized it as one of the "110 Mary's" from the database list he had provided—one Mary for whom I had been unable to locate a telephone number. Within a few hours of my call, Ron found my Mary's correct telephone number and called me with the incredible news. I sat down to smoke a cigarette and gather my wits. My husband, who'd lived for two years with the daily physical and emotional intensity of the search, couldn't believe it. He said, "Aren't you going to CALL her?!" Although I'd had to gather my courage many times before in talking to the two hundred or more women who might have been Mary, never had one seemed so likely to be the right woman. I wanted to think of the "right" questions to ask, to determine conclusively whether or not this woman was indeed my mother, in the event she denied it. Finally, I realized my courage wasn't going to grow by waiting, and that I would have to trust that the right words would come from my mouth. I dialed Mary's number.

MAKING CONTACT

A soft-spoken woman answered the telephone. I asked, "Is this Mary?" and, when she said she was, I proceeded to ask her the same questions I'd asked at least 200 people before. I told her, "I'm looking for a woman named Mary who used to live in Nashville." She said, "I did," and I said, "and also lived in Memphis," and she said, "I did." I asked, "Was your father's name Henry?" and she said "It was," and volunteered, "and my mother's name was Mary Lois." There was no doubt about it, I knew this was my Mary at last. I said, "Well, my name's Patricia." Her gentle voice became even softer, "My Patricia?" I told her yes, and started crying. She said, "Oh, this is wonderful." She said she had hoped and hoped that I would find her, and said, "You must have read my mind." She told me that for the previous several weeks she had been gathering together all her photographs, of her family, and of herself, of me as a baby and toddler. Somehow she had a feeling she would need to get this memorabilia together. She said she had promised the orphanage that she would never interfere in my life, and that she didn't feel it was right for her to look for her children and possibly disrupt our lives. I talked with Mary for 45 minutes, and then told her Carol wanted to call her also. I was delighted to call Carol and give her, as my first sister-to-sister gift, our mother's phone number.

Carol talked with Mary that night, and then drove to Mary's home town on June 24 to meet her, sharing this beautiful experience with me by cell-phone. I heard her following the directions she had been given to Mary's house, getting lost, asking strangers on the street for directions. I heard her when she first saw Mary and listened to her sob when she first embraced our mother. She handed the phone to Mary, who repeated the phrase I think I heard most often from her, "Oh, this is wonderful. This is wonderful." Carol drove Mary to Memphis to meet her immediate family, and on June 26th to Nashville to meet my plane.

The Bureaucracy of Searching

by G. William Troxler

G. William Troxler learned at a late age that he had been adopted. As Troxler explains in the following narrative, the discovery was accidental and came about when he was engaged in a routine request for his birth certificate. Maryland, the state where Troxler was adopted, has a law that closes the birth record of adoptees. These records cannot be accessed without a court order, and the information cannot be analyzed without the assistance of a third party intermediary. When Troxler attempted to access his birth certificate, he was denied and told that the reason for the denial was probably due to the fact that he had been adopted.

After dealing with the initial shock of learning the truth about his birth, Troxler decided to begin searching for his birth mother. In his story, Troxler explains the frustration at having to deal with bureaucracy, red tape, and possible criminalization in order to merely find out more about his birth parents. After three years, he says, he was able to gain access to his adoption records. However he has been unable to locate his birth mother. Troxler claims that he will continue his search because he believes in the importance of knowing the truth about his origins.

After serving Maryland's Capitol College for twenty-seven years, G. William Troxler retired from his post as president in June 2003. Among his distinctions, Troxler has been inducted into the Washington Academy of Sciences and was appointed by the governor to serve eight years as chairman of the Maryland Apprenticeship and Training Council.

I knew the document in my hands was a lie. It was too neat, too stark. It lacked the official signature. When I asked the clerk at the Vital Records Office for an explanation, she said that this was an amended birth certificate. The original document was under seal of

G. William Troxler, "The Search for Marianne," *Newsweek,* vol. 127, May 27, 1996. Copyright © 1996 by Newsweek, Inc. All rights reserved. Reproduced by permission.

court. "But why?" I protested. I'm a responsible citizen—Vietnam veteran, college president, trustee of numerous boards and gubernatorial commissions. The clerk's answer was disconcertingly matter-of-fact: "Probably you're adopted." That is how, at the age of 46, I came to learn that I am unrelated to the couple I know and love as Mom and Dad.

When I entered that government office, I was certain of my identity. I knew that I was born in Washington, D.C., on Feb. 25, 1947. My parents were Lurline Pettus and George William Troxler. I was descended from Johann Gabor Troxler, who had left Bavaria in 1719 and entered America through the port of New Orleans. The family had taken root in the South—Alabama and North Carolina, to be specific. I could recite to you who among my ancestors fought in the Civil War, their major battles and who died at Point Lookout prisoner-of-war camp.

A month later, all that remained of my heritage was the date and place of my birth. Soon the date was also in question, although I learned that my mother's name was probably Marianne. The hospital that provided my baby footprints denied that I had been born there. The attorney who did the legal work for my adoption had no record of it. The physician who had delivered me was deceased, and his files had been destroyed.

SEARCHING IN VAIN

Nearly three years after my encounter with truth in that government office, I have tried everything possible to find Marianne. I took an eight-month sabbatical to pursue the quest full time. I have scrutinized tax records, birth certificates, divorce filings, old newspapers and high-school yearbooks in about 100 counties—on a good day, scanning 200,000 handwritten records. I do not recommend this activity unless myopia is one of your significant life goals. I have written more than 3,000 letters to individuals who might know of my mother. The Internet has yielded no answers. Neither has the Library of Congress, nor the Family History Center of the Mormon Church. I have hired a private investigator. All in vain.

It is hard to convey what it feels like to search. I am daily reminded of Kafka's novel "The Trial." The tale pits the protagonist against a baffling legal bureaucracy. He is unsuccessful in trying to communicate with the authorities and ultimately cannot receive justice. He is charged and tormented, but never convicted, never sentenced, never acquitted, never told of the charges against him. That may be as accurate a description of the search experience as I can provide.

I sit across a desk from a man with my adoption record in his hands. There can't be more than a dozen pages in the slim file, but every word of the information is about me. He decides what I may see, what I may know about myself. When I ask him for the file, he tells me he cannot let me see it under the laws of Maryland, the state where I was adopted. When I tell him I want to know facts about my birth, he tells me that my birth is none of my business.

IGNORANCE IS NOT BLISS

Many friends have tried to dissuade me from looking. "I know who you are," they say. How comforting. Everyone else knows me better than I do. "Your mother may not want to be found," they say. But I know that she had some misgivings about putting me up for adoption. On several occasions when I was an infant, Marianne paced up and down our sidewalk, or sat in the car outside, hoping for a glimpse of me. "Ignorance is bliss," my friends tell me. But in the case of adoptees, ignorance could be a death sentence, lurking unseen in a medical history. "Suppose you find bad news?" they say. The news may be bad, but it is my news. I vacate my humanity if I allow a government-crafted fiction of my life to supplant the truth.

A sympathetic judge in Maryland finally allowed me to examine my adoption file. He even gave me copies of my Order of Adoption and the Consent Decree by which Marianne signed me away. These are ordinary pieces of 8-by-11 paper. Still, I can't look at them without my palms sweating. These pages changed my life. The consent decree is particularly poignant. My birthmother speaks of me as "indigent, neglected, destitute and homeless"—a sea of words that are very dramatic. Even more striking to me is her signature—Marianne—at the bottom of the page. Her scrawled name may be the only contact beyond infancy that I will ever have with her. I know even less about my biological father. The file lists his name cryptically as "Jones (?)." His religion, as "Gentile."

Now that Maryland has opened my adoption record, I am appealing to the courts in Washington, D.C., to unseal my birth certificate. Why should it be so difficult? Nearly all of you who read this can obtain copies of your birth certificates. It is a trivial act of information retrieval. Your name and a small fee presented to the right office and, poof, there appears a single page of information you already knew. But I am an unequal citizen under the law.

You may think that my concerns are increasingly irrelevant in a society where out-of-wedlock birth no longer carries a stigma. Wrong. It is true that the adoption process is more open now than when I was a child. Adoptive families generally receive a medical file, and the two sets of parents may even exchange pictures. However, the notion still remains enshrined in law that the birth records should be sealed in perpetuity. Under the proposed Uniform Adoption Act, there are even efforts in state legislatures to criminalize the act of searching for one's birth relatives. Even though my adoption file came to me through legitimate sources, I would be guilty of a felony for possessing it. If Maryland should pass this law, I could be subject to a $10,000 penalty for the simple act of seeking my birthmother.

Why do I continue? It's not that I need a mother to nurture me. I'm nearly 50. But I've spent my entire adult life telling my students that truth matters. I need to learn the truth about my origins—and I hope to do so while Marianne is still alive.

Searching Brings an Adoptive Mother and Daughter Closer

by Marybeth Lambe and Emma Rose Levy

At the time the following narrative was written, Emma Rose Levy was a thirteen-year-old adopted daughter of Marybeth Lambe and her husband. In the following narrative Emma Rose and Marybeth provide an account of Levy's success in reuniting with her birth mother.

Lambe explains that her daughter became curious about the whereabouts of her birth mother when she was six years old. Aware of the importance of her daughter's knowing the truth about her birth parents, Lambe supported Levy in her search. Two years passed when finally the adoption agency that had placed Levy indicated that Levy's birth mother had been found and contacted. Arrangements were made for the two to meet, and the reunion was a happy experience for everyone involved.

Lambe stresses her belief that adopted children must know their origins in order to achieve peace. However, she feels that adoptive parents should let the children conduct the search at their own pace. She is happy for her daughter's discovery and is glad that Levy was cautious and patient in her search. For Lambe, it is exciting to have "a broken chain fixed, a circle formed."

Marybeth Lambe is a family physician and writer. Emma Rose Levy is a student in secondary school.

Marybeth: Most adoptees who search for their birthparents do so as adults. Yet the questions that propel them have been percolating for some time. Even as children, adoptees feel a tug to learn about where they came from. They need to know why, how, and above all, who.

Our adopted children have wondered aloud about their birth

families from the time they were very young. It's unlikely we'll ever connect with the birth families of our Chinese children. But meeting her birthmother has always been a possibility for our American-born daughter, Emma Rose. As she grew older, it became a longing, then an imperative, and finally, a quest.

This is the story of her journey.

Emma Rose: I am 13, and I was adopted when I was 4 months old. I don't remember that day, but my parents have told me how my hands attached to theirs and how much laughter I had to share. As I got older, I realized that I was African American but the rest of my nine family members were not. I wondered about the woman who had created me.

Marybeth: I wondered, too, had she been able to move on with her life, or was she filled with regret? Was she well? As an adoptive mom, I have always felt a bond with my children's birthmothers. I wished I could tell them what I had whispered in my heart for so long: "If you could see your child, you would behold her with wonder. I hope my parenting makes you proud."

We had few facts to pass on to Emma as she grew—only that her mother had made an adoption plan. After the adoption, we sent updates and photographs to the agency in hope that Emma's birthmother would receive them. We were told she had never made contact again.

Emma Rose: Every day I would fantasize, could I be the child of Tyra Banks or Jennifer Lopez? Would she come to claim me one day? Then I would be famous too. My mom always said that anything was a possibility, and it was good to wonder and dream. She guessed my birthmom was beautiful because I am pretty, and that perhaps she had graceful hands and feet like mine. She said my birthmom had beauty on the inside too, where it really counts, because she had made sure that her daughter had a family and a good life.

DESIRE TO KNOW

Marybeth: Beginning at age 6, Emma spoke of her desire to learn more about her first mother. Even if her mother was troubled, or the story harsh or sad, Emma needed to know her origins. As she neared her tenth birthday, we talked with social workers, therapists, and adult adoptees. All felt she could handle the process and the outcome, even at her young age. We decided it was time to allow Emma to search.

It was hard not to step in and push the process. I wanted to know this shadow mother, this woman who shared a daughter with me. But an adoptive parent cannot search. Adult adoptees emphasize that searching is about regaining control, making choices, and coming to terms with loss. Only Emma Rose could determine the speed of her search, her path, her stops and starts. We could be her anchors, but we were bystanders on the journey.

Two years passed as Emma Rose searched. With my help, she contacted the adoption agency many times, and sent letters in the hope that her birthmother might receive them. At last, an agency worker gave her the news we were hoping for. She had been able to contact Emma's birthmom.

Emma Rose: When we heard that my birthmother had been found, Mom and I sent an e-mail to the agency and asked if she would want to contact me. I became very anxious. Suppose she didn't want to know me? Finally the response came that my biological mother would love to start a relationship! They also told me her name: Movale Tillman. I remember reading her beautiful name and clenching my mom's hand with excitement.

Then the moment! I asked my mom to call. My mom and birthmom shared stories and tears. My mom told Movale that she had always been in our hearts, and that she was part of our family. Then she handed the phone to me. Movale said she loved me and asked how my life was going. I stayed strong, without crying, and told her I was just fine and that I loved her too. It was a strange and wonderful day. This was who I came from!

Marybeth: It was a strange and wonderful day. I was relieved by the warm welcome Movale had given Emma Rose. I was delighted to know she was healthy and that her life was good. Unexpectedly, I felt a thrill at this new connection. A broken chain had been fixed, a circle formed.

Many adoptees describe that first contact as a dreamlike, honeymoon event. Later, for many, the relationship becomes rockier. It's hard to hammer out new relationships, but our family has been lucky. Two years later, the bloom of joy is still with us.

THE BIG TRIP

Emma Rose: Movale and mom and I talked on the phone for several months. I learned I had two brothers and a sister. When I felt ready, my dad took me to Atlanta to meet my birth family. On the airplane

I went into the bathroom constantly to be sure I looked OK. I started to get nervous and scared—scared that my birthmother wouldn't like me, or would think I was weird. As I walked off the plane, my gorgeous birthmother and sister greeted me with flowers. This time, I couldn't hold back my tears.

Marybeth: As Emma Rose boarded the plane for Georgia, I felt anxious. My daughter was marching into unknown territory. Suppose she was frightened? Would she understand Movale's reasons for placing her for adoption? And what if Emma preferred her birth family to us? We are large and noisy and chaotic. How would we stack up during this long-awaited reunion?

Yes, there were risks. But to prevent Movale and Emma Rose from exploring their history and their future would have been even riskier. Parenting is about the long haul. At 12 years of age, Emma was ready for this visit. I needed to keep my feelings in check.

The visit was everything we could have hoped for. Movale showed great courage and love. She introduced Emma to the extended family and spoke openly and honestly with her. We learned whom Emma takes after in her looks, her petite stature, and some aspects of her personality. Since the visit, through letters and phone calls, we have come to know each other even better, and we're planning a reunion this summer.

Emma Rose: Now you know the advantage of two families. Both families didn't only answer my questions; they answered my prayers. Mark and Marybeth are my parents by heart. They're the ones who feed me, tuck me in at night, and hold me when I cry. Movale is my first mother; she gave me the love to grow. I am who I am because of all of them.

Marybeth: The decision to search is hard. But it's not ours to make. We must put aside our worries, both foolish and the real. Our children shouldn't be made to feel they have betrayed us when they choose to search. They haven't betrayed us. They simply need to feel whole.

Emma Rose: I know that not everyone's story ends so well. But I'd spent so much time wondering: How could my birthmom let me go? Now I know she didn't; she's still a part of me. I may not be a movie star's daughter (darn it), but I know who I am for real. I finally have my story.

My Birth Mother Was Not What I Expected

by Susina Damaschina

When she learned that her adoptive father had copies of her adoption records, Susina Damaschina decided to look for her birth mother. After several years of searching, Damaschina finally had the information she needed in order to make contact with her birth mother. In the following article, Damaschina gives an account of the rocky relationship that came as a result of reuniting with her long lost parent.

According to Damaschina, her first meeting with her birth mother was pleasant, but she recognized that there were things about her mother that were both quirky and slightly off-putting. What she initially accepted as eccentricity, however, eventually became much more damaging to their relationship. After several months of trying to understand her mother's behavior, Damaschina let the relationship cool for both their sakes. She ultimately realized that her birth mother would never be a significant part of her life.

L ike most adoptees, I often wondered and fantasized about who my biological parents might be. It never really occurred to me to search. The whole idea must have been taboo since I can't remember it entering my mind as a child or even as a teenager. I often wondered if I would ever just magically meet up with my birthparents, and for a time I entertained the notion that my aunt was my birthmother. When, in a drunken moment of desperation I finally questioned her about it, she had the nerve to reply, "No, but if I were, I wouldn't tell you." What an a—hole. Then and there I knew she couldn't be my birthmother. My birthmother would smile beatifically and welcome me with open arms. She would accept me as I am, be proud of my accomplishments and enrich my life with her great knowledge. My birthmother would never say anything so harsh and so rude. Little did I know. . . .

One day, soon after my 18th birthday, I was eating dinner at my father's apartment. Somehow the subject of my adoption came up and my Dad said that he had the adoption papers with my "original name" on them. Naturally I went ballistic jumping around like an idiot and shouting "Where?! Where?! What is it?! What is it?!" My Dad got a big kick out of this and tried to draw it out but eventually he went into a drawer and handed me some yellowed papers. It was the decree of adoption and there typed in bold black capitals was my "original name." My Dad told me that I could go to the agency and get non-identifying information. I think he may have been as curious as I was. The next day I made an appointment.

It took another seven years for me to embark wholeheartedly on my search. Soon after I finished school I decided that it was time to find a husband and start a family of my own. It was then that, like so many others, I decided to search in earnest.

WAITING FOR THE RIGHT MOMENT

I will spare you the particulars of my search. Suffice it to say that I was completely obsessed with it for a year and a half. After about six months in full-throttle obsesso-mode I found a grandparent. It was a wonderful experience except that she didn't want me to contact my birthmother. She said it was a painful episode in her life that no one spoke of after it happened. She said some family members didn't even know about it. She said that I shouldn't want to rock the boat. She even said that she would put our correspondence in a locked vault and that she had instructed her lawyer to have them destroyed upon her demise. What the f— had I gotten myself into?! At that time I was too caught up in it all to really consider the implication of her attitudes. I was scheming behind the scenes to find bio-mom. Using some very sneaky homespun tactics, I tracked her down and discovered her name, address, phone number, place of work and work number. Not wanting to betray my grandmother (who had no idea of what I had done), I sat on this information for nine whole months. When my grandmother came out to visit me a year after I had contacted her, she still didn't know that I had this information. I would just look at it. Didn't do anything with it. Didn't even call and hang up. Just sat and waited.

As you know, the day came when I couldn't sit on it anymore. One sunny June morning I must have had spring fever or something because I woke up knowing I would talk to my birthmother that day.

Not to sound mystical or anything, but something just clicked and I knew that would be the day. I went to work but I couldn't concentrate. At 11:00 I would call her at work. And I did. And she freaked. I mean, she was happy. She dropped the phone and I could hear her screaming "My daughter! My daughter! It's my daughter! She found me!" So I started crying like an idiot on the public phone in the hallway at my work. Later I saw that my mascara had run all down my cheeks. I should have put on the waterproof!

A PLEASANT REUNION

Biomom was on a plane out to see me the same week. I got all prettied up, but with no makeup so that she could see what I look like au natural. My girlfriend drove me to the airport to meet her and I twiddled my thumbs and tapped my feet for about an hour waiting for her plane to arrive. When it finally did she was one of the first ones out. I smiled politely and she shook my hand. It was all quite civil really. No hugging, no sobbing, no starry-eyed soul-searching stares of long-lost recognition. Just sort of pleasant.

As we left to return to my place I started picking up pieces of evidence which would eventually lead me to believe that my biomom was a freak. She struck up inane conversations with about 5 different strangers on the way from the terminal to the baggage claim to the car. She handed out stickers to several children. She took down addresses. She accosted people speaking foreign languages. At that time I was a bit star-struck and I thought "Oh, how delightfully eccentric she is!" Yeah. Right.

When we got back to my apartment, I showed her around but she was much more concerned with telling me every detail of her life since she was born until that very day. Neither of us slept that first night. She confessed all manner of things to me. Things I didn't particularly want to hear, but hey, if it made her feel better. . . .

The second day she let loose her first real bombshell." You know, I have to tell you something. I named the wrong guy as your father." Er, OK. So tell me about Tom. It didn't hit me straight away that some other poor slob had been running around all these years thinking he had a daughter somewhere out there. Later, when that other poor slob wrote me a letter I realized how stupid my biomom had been. Oh well, we're all entitled to mistakes. Problem is, biomom made a few too many.

The next time I saw biomom was a few months later at my wedding. My parents had invited the bios and their spouses and everyone got along very well. Biomom and biodad danced together at the wedding which was very scary to watch, the least because she is an Amazonian 6'2" and biodad is a stout 5'5". Everyone was on their best behavior.

The real trouble began in the months following my wedding. I got pregnant pretty much right away and biomom started calling frequently and writing long-winded letters about how Jesus had saved her soul from mortal perdition. She sent me tapes on how to attain salvation. She sent me a personally inscribed Bible. She even sent booklets on how the theory of evolution was "The Devil's Monkey Business." When she called she would always ask that I allow her to pray for me over the phone. She prayed in tongues, which basically means she spouted gibberish in a very solemn tone and then said "Amen." I felt obligated to say "Amen" too. So gradually I was getting sucked into her influence. I had never been a member of any organized religion in my life and this whole scene was very new to me. Basically I wanted her acceptance. She hadn't seemed very interested in my past or interests or accomplishments. She was just fixated on herself and on Jesus. And on sucking other people into her Jesus-trap. That's what I started to realize all her aggressive solicitation of strangers was about. Unfortunately I was still under her spell.

When I was four months pregnant I went out to visit her by myself. Like a needy child, I decided to accept Jesus to please her. She took me to her church, paraded me before a bunch of beaming, over-fed fundamentalists and was very warm and loving with me generally. She even took me to a Christian "therapy" session during which I tricked myself into thinking that Jesus himself had pulled 100 yards of rotten intestines out of my body. Hey, maybe I'm just as nutty as she is!

But not quite. A few months after I returned home I realized what I was doing. I was lying to myself and to my biomom so as to gain her acceptance. I was scared to tell her how I really felt. She was so happy that I had found Jesus! Who knows how she would react? The charade could only go on for so long though. One day she called me and I just told her point blank that I didn't believe in Jesus and I had done it just to please her. She tried to talk me out of it, but I stood my ground. Everything was downhill from there. No more frequent phone calls, no more letters, no more elaborate packages in the mail. I wonder if she felt betrayed. I wonder if she understands the irony of how she treated me.

FALLING OUT AND FORGIVENESS

The next time I saw biomom was when my first son was four months old. She came out for an obligatory visit and basically made my life hell. The first night she broke down crying and begged me to forgive her. For what? She told me that she would have aborted me had it been legal. She told me that she had even gone to the very door of the abortion clinic but turned back at the last minute because she feared for her own life (abortion was illegal back then). I was very understanding and told her that of course I forgave her. But the bitch wouldn't stop there. Then she told me that she tried several "natural" methods of aborting me, obviously none of which worked. Fine, whatever. Then she told me that I was a big mistake and that God had punished her for sleeping around before marriage. Oy f—ing vey! Still, I was patient. Then she started crying even more and told me that I had ruined her life! And there I was, patting her head, wiping away her tears and telling her "It's all right, it's all right." But it wasn't all right. From that point on the only feelings I could have for this woman were pity and disgust.

These themes were the topic of several subsequent conversations, all initiated by my biomom and all ending with me saying "Of course I forgive you. Stop torturing yourself." I still can't figure out why she insisted on repeating these hurtful things over and over to me unless they were designed to guilt me into accepting Jesus or something. Whatever the reason may be, I have now decided that I simply don't like her and I will be happier without her in my life. Being basically compassionate, I will send her the obligatory birthday and Christmas cards, but that's it. And she's lucky she's getting that. Just as I'm lucky to be alive.

The editors have compiled the following list of organizations concerned with the issues debated in this book. The descriptions are derived from materials provided by the organizations. All have publications or information available for interested readers. The list was compiled on the date of publication of the present volume; the information provided here may change. Be aware that many organizations take several weeks or longer to respond to inquiries, so allow as much time as possible.

ABOLISH ADOPTION

PO Box 401, Palm Desert, CA 92261
e-mail: info@abolishadoption.com • Web site: www.abolishadoption.com

Abolish Adoption is an organization that petitions to end the practice of adoption. Its members believe that adoption is not in a child's best interests and violates human rights. Abolish Adoption also campaigns for open adoption record laws. The organization sells *The Ultimate Search Book: Worldwide Adoption, Genealogy, and Other Search Secrets* by Lori Carangelo.

AMERICAN ADOPTION CONGRESS (AAC)

PO Box 42730, Washington, DC 20015
(202) 483-3399
e-mail: patdenn@primenet.com
Web site: www.americanadoptioncongress.org

AAC is an educational network that promotes openness and honesty in adoption. It advocates adoption reform, including the opening of adoption records, and seeks to develop plans for alternative models for adoption. It addresses the needs of adult adoptees who are searching for their birth families. AAC publishes the quarterly *Search/Support Group Directory*.

ASSOCIATION FOR RESEARCH IN INTERNATIONAL ADOPTION (ARIA)

University of South Alabama College of Nursing, Community Mental Health
Springhill Area Campus, Mobile, AL 36688-0002
(251) 434-3448 • fax: (251) 434-3995
e-mail: info@adoption-research.org • Web site: www.adoption-research.org

The ARIA Web site, maintained by the University of South Alabama College of Nursing, is an online clearinghouse for research relevant to the international adoption community. The site also contains links for adoptive parents wishing to learn more about the issues involved in adopting a foreign child.

BASTARD NATION

PO Box 271672, Houston, TX 77277-1672
(415) 704-3166
e-mail: members@bastards.org • Web site: www.bastards.org

Bastard Nation is an adoptees' rights organization that campaigns to legalize adopted adults' access to records that pertain to their historical, genetic, and legal identity. It publishes the newsletter *Bastard Quarterly.*

CHILD WELFARE LEAGUE OF AMERICA (CWLA)

440 First St. NW, Suite 310, Third Floor, Washington, DC 20001
(202) 638-2952 • fax: (202) 638-4004
Web site: www.cwla.org

CWLA is a social welfare organization concerned with setting standards for welfare and human services agencies. It encourages research on all aspects of adoption. It publishes *Child Welfare: A Journal of Policy, Practice, and Program.*

CONCERNED UNITED BIRTHPARENTS (CUB)

PO Box 503475, San Diego, CA 92150-3475
(800) 822-2777 • fax: (858) 435-4863
e-mail: info@CUBirthparents.org • Web site: www.cubirthparents.org

CUB provides assistance to birth parents, works to open adoption records, and seeks to develop alternatives to the current adoption system. It helps women considering the placement of a child for adoption make informed choices and seeks to prevent unnecessary separation of families by adoption. CUB publishes the monthly *CUB Communicator.*

EVAN B. DONALDSON ADOPTION INSTITUTE

525 Broadway, Sixth Floor, New York, NY 10012
(212) 925-4089 • fax: (775) 796-6592
e-mail: info@adoptioninstitute.org • Web site: www.adoptioninstitute.org

The Evan B. Donaldson Adoption Institute works with lawmakers, the media, adoption professionals, and public education services to make the issue of adoption more visible. The institute also publishes a series of books dealing with the ethics of adoption.

FAMILIES FOR PRIVATE ADOPTION (FPA)

PO Box 6375, Washington, DC 20015
(202) 722-0338
e-mail: ffpa@email.com • Web site: www.ffpa.org

FPA assists people considering private adoption (adoption without the use of an adoption agency). In addition to providing information on adoption procedures and legal concerns, it offers referrals to doctors, lawyers, and social workers. FPA publishes the quarterly *FPA Bulletin.*

NATIONAL ADOPTION CENTER (NAC)

1500 Walnut St., Suite 701, Philadelphia, PA 19102
(215) 735-9988
e-mail: nac@adopt.org • Web site: www.adopt.org

NAC promotes the adoption of older, disabled, and minority children and of siblings who seek to be placed together. It provides information, registration, family recruitment, and matching referral services for children and prospective adoptive parents. It publishes the semiannual *National Adoption Center Newsletter.*

NATIONAL ADOPTION INFORMATION CLEARINGHOUSE (NAIC)

330 C St. SW, Washington, DC 20447
(888) 251-0075 or (703) 352-3488 • fax: (703) 385-3206
e-mail: naic@caliber.com • Web site: http://naic.acf.hhs.gov

The National Adoption Information Clearinghouse is a service provided by the U.S. Department of Health and Human Services. NAIC distributes publications on all aspects of adoption, including infant and international adoption, the adoption of children with special needs, and pertinent state and federal laws. For researchers, it provides a computerized information database containing titles and abstracts of books, articles, and program reports on adoption.

NATIONAL ASSOCIATION OF BLACK SOCIAL WORKERS (NABSW)

1220 Eleventh St. NW, Suite 2, Washington, DC 20001
(202) 589-1850 • fax: (202) 589-1853
e-mail: ssw@unc.edu • Web site: http://ssw.unc.edu/professional/NABSW.html

NABSW seeks to support, develop, and sponsor programs and projects serving the interests of black communities. It is committed to a policy of same-race adoptions, promoting adoption of black children by black adoptive parents. NABSW publishes the annual *Black Caucus.*

NATIONAL COALITION FOR CHILD PROTECTION REFORM (NCCPR)

53 Skyhill Rd., Suite 202, Alexandria, VA 22314
(703) 212-2006
e-mail: info@NCCPR.org • Web site: www.nccpr.org

NCCPR is a group of professionals who work to improve the child welfare system by trying to change policies concerning child abuse, foster care, and family preservation. NCCPR advocates for systemic reform and does not provide advice in dealing with individual cases. It publishes issue papers on family preservation and foster care.

NATIONAL COUNCIL FOR ADOPTION (NCFA)

225 N. Washington St., Alexandria, VA 22314-2561
(703) 299-6633 • fax: (703) 299-6004
e-mail: ncfa@adoptioncouncil.org • Web site: www.ncfa-usa.org

Representing volunteer agencies, adoptive parents, adoptees, and birth parents, NCFA works to protect the institution of adoption and to ensure the confidentiality of all involved in the adoption process. It strives for adoption regulations that will maintain the protection of birth parents, children, and adoptive parents. Its biweekly newsletter, *Memo*, provides updates on state and federal legislative and regulatory changes affecting adoption.

NATIONAL COUNCIL FOR SINGLE ADOPTIVE PARENTS (NCSAP)

PO Box 55, Wharton, NJ 07885
(202) 966-6367
e-mail: ncsap@hotmail.com • Web site: www.adopting.org/ncsap.html

Formerly the Committee for Single Adoptive Parents (CSAP), NCSAP is an information clearinghouse for singles who have adopted or who wish to adopt a child. It refers interested individuals to local parent support groups and provides names of agencies that work with single adoptive parents. It publishes the *Handbook for Single Adoptive Parents* and a directory.

NATIONAL ORGANIZATION FOR BIRTHFATHERS AND ADOPTION REFORM (NOBAR)

PO Box 50, Punta Gorda, FL 33951-0050
(813) 637-7477

NOBAR is an advocacy group for men affected by adoption (including birth fathers of adoptees, divorced fathers whose children are or may be adopted by stepfathers, single fathers, and adoptive fathers). The organization promotes social policies and laws that protect the individual rights of those involved in adoptions. It also works for the unrestricted opening of adoption records for birth parents and adoptees. NOBAR publishes *Birthfathers' Advocate*, a monthly newsletter.

NORTH AMERICAN COUNCIL ON ADOPTABLE CHILDREN (NACAC)

970 Raymond Ave., Suite 106, St. Paul, MN 55114-1149
(651) 644-3036 • fax: (651) 644-9848
e-mail: info@nacac.org • Web site: www.nacac.org

NACAC, an adoption advocacy organization, emphasizes special needs adoption, keeps track of adoption activities in each state, and promotes reform in adoption policies. NACAC publishes *Adoptalk* quarterly.

RAINBOWKIDS

1821 Commercial Dr., Suite S, Harvey, LA 70058
e-mail: letters@rainbowkids.com • Web site: www.rainbowkids.com

RainbowKids, the oldest and largest international adoption organization, helps families of internationally adopted children learn about international adoption, offers support during the adoption process, and provides resources to assist a newly adopted child adjust to his or her new family. The Web site has an archive of past articles written about subjects ranging from regular international adoption to adoption of special needs and older children.

RESOLVE, INC.

7910 Woodmont Ave., Suite 1350, Bethesda, MD 20814
(301) 652-8585 • fax: (301) 652-9375
e-mail: resolveinc@aol.com • Web site: www.resolve.org

Resolve, Inc., is a nationwide information network serving the needs of men and women dealing with infertility and adoption issues. It publishes fact sheets and a quarterly national newsletter containing articles, medical information, and book reviews.

REUNITE, INC.

PO Box 694, Reynoldsburg, OH 43068

Reunite, Inc., promotes adoption reform and assists in searches for birth parents and adopted children. It publishes a brochure titled *Reunite*.

WEB SITES

ADOPTING.COM

www.adopting.com

Adopting.com is a resource Web site offering information for prospective adopters. Included on the site are links to several national adoption agencies, lawyers, letters to birth parents, and photo listings of children who are up for adoption.

ADOPTION.COM

http://adoption.com

Adoption.com is a Web-based network of adoption organizations. This collective site features profiles of prospective adoptive parents and adoptable children. It also posts articles that address adoption issues such as unplanned pregnancy, international adoption, and adoption reunions. Several publications are offered at this site, such as *2001 Adoption Guide* and *Adoption Today* magazine.

ADOPTIVE FAMILIES OF AMERICA (AFA)

www.adoptivefamilies.com

AFA serves as an umbrella organization supporting adoptive parents groups. It provides problem-solving assistance and information about the challenges of adoption to members of adoptive and prospective adoptive families. It also seeks to create opportunities for successful adoptive placement and promotes the health and welfare of children without permanent homes. AFA publishes the bimonthly magazine *Adoptive Families* (formerly *Ours* magazine).

BOOKS

Julie Jarrell Bailey and Lynn N. Giddens, *Adoption Reunion Survival Guide: Preparing Yourself for the Search, Reunion, and Beyond*. Oakland, CA: New Harbinger, 2001.

Tracy Barr and Katrina Carlisle, *Adoption for Dummies*. Hoboken, NJ: Wiley, 2003.

Randi G. Barrow, *Somebody's Child: Stories from the Private Files of an Adoption Attorney*. New York: Perigee, 2002.

Elizabeth Bartholet, *Family Bonds: Adoption, Infertility, and the New World of Child Production*. Boston: Beacon, 1999.

Susan L. Burns, *Fast Track Adoption: The Faster, Safer Way to Privately Adopt a Baby*. New York: St. Martin's Griffin, 2003.

E. Wayne Carp, *Adoption in America: Historical Perspectives*. Ann Arbor: University of Michigan Press, 2004.

———, *Adoption Politics: Bastard Nation and Ballot Initiative 58*. Lawrence: University Press of Kansas, 2004.

Amy Coughlin and Caryn Abramowitz, *Cross Cultural Adoption: How to Answer Questions from Family, Friends, and Community*. Washington, DC: Lifeline, 2004.

Sherie Eldridge, *Twenty Things Adopted Kids Wish Their Adoptive Parents Knew*. New York: Dell, 1999.

Hawley Fogg-Davis, *The Ethics of Transracial Adoption*. Ithaca, NY: Cornell University Press, 2002.

Karen J. Foli and John R. Thompson, *The Post-Adoption Blues: Overcoming the Unforseen Challenges of Adoption*. New York: St. Martin's, 2004.

Deborah D. Gray, *Attaching in Adoption: Practical Tools for Today's Parents*. Indianapolis: Perspectives, 2002.

Kay Ann Johnson and Amy Klatzkin, *Wanting a Daughter, Needing a Son: Abandonment, Adoption, and Orphanage Care in China.* St. Paul, MN: Yeong & Yeong, 2004.

Gail Kinn, *Be My Baby: Parents and Children Talk About Adoption.* New York: Artisan, 2000.

Betty Jean Lifton, *Lost and Found: The Adoption Experience.* New York: Perennial, 1988.

Jeanne Warren Lindsay, *Pregnant? Adoption Is an Option: Making an Adoption Plan for a Child.* Buena Park, CA: Morning Glory, 1997.

Cynthia D. Martin and Dru Martin Groves, *Beating the Adoption Odds: Using Your Head and Your Heart to Adopt.* San Diego: Harcourt, Brace, 1998.

Kevin McGarry, *Fatherhood for Gay Men: An Emotional and Practical Guide to Becoming a Gay Dad.* New York: Harrington Park, 2003.

Lois Ruskai Melina and Sharon Kaplan Roszia, *The Open Adoption Experience: A Complete Guide for Adoptive and Birth Families—From Making the Decision Through the Child's Growing Years.* New York: HarperPerennial, 1993.

Adam Pertman, *Adoption Nation: How the Adoption Revolution Is Transforming America.* New York: Basic, 2001.

Grace Robinson, *Older Child Adoption.* New York: Crossroad, 1998.

Marlou Russell, *Adoption Wisdom: A Guide to the Issues and Feelings of Adoption.* Santa Monica, CA: Broken Branch Production, 1996.

Kathleen Silber and Patricia Martinez Dorner, *Children of Open Adoption and Their Families.* San Antonio, TX: Corona, 1990.

Joanne Wolf Small, *The Adoption Mystique.* Bloomington, IN: Authorhouse, 2004.

Joe Sol and Karen Wilson Buterbaugh, *Adoption Healing: A Path to Recovery for Mothers Who Lost Children to Adoption.* Baltimore: Gateway, 2003.

Gail Steinberg and Beth Hall, *Inside Transracial Adoption.* Indianapolis: Perspectives, 2000.

Mary Watkins and Susan Fisher, *Talking with Young Children About Adoption*. New Haven, CT: Yale University Press, 1995.

PERIODICALS

Matthew Anderson and Oliver Conroy, "Foster Care Kids Are Happier Without Adoption," *New York Amsterdam News*, May 29, 2003.

Devon Brooks and Sheryl Goldberg, "Gay and Lesbian Adoptive and Foster Care Placements: Can They Meet the Needs of Waiting Children?" *Social Work*, April 2001.

Devon Brooks, Sigrid James, and Richard P. Barth, "Preferred Characteristics of Children in Need of Adoption: Is There a Demand for Available Foster Children?" *Social Service Review*, December 2002.

Christina Cheackalos and Ron Arias, "Happier by the Dozen," *People*, November 4, 2002.

Steve Christian, "Healing the Hole in the Heart," *State Legislatures*, December 2002.

Kim Clark and Nancy Shute, "The Adoption Maze," *U.S. News & World Report*, March 12, 2001.

Sarah Corbett, "Where Do Babies Come From?" *New York Times Magazine*, June 16, 2002.

Alyssa Burrell Cowan, "New Strategies to Promote the Adoption of Older Children Out of Foster Care," *Children & Youth Services Review*, November 2004.

Janet Crawley, "The Transformation of Angelina Jolie," *Biography*, October 2003.

Terry Eastland, "The Forgotten Option," *Human Life Review*, Winter 2003.

Amy Engeler, "Last Chance Kids," *Good Housekeeping*, September 2003.

Sue Ferguson, "Hard-Sell Adoption," *Maclean's*, July 26, 2004.

Thomas Fields-Meyer and Strawberry, "Our Twenty-Five Sons," *People*, February 2, 2004.

Nikitta A. Foston, "Small Miracles: New Hope for Black Adoptions," *Ebony*, November 2003.

Lisa Gubernick, "Adoptees Search for Their Roots," *Wall Street Journal*, March 20, 2002.

Alexandra N. Helper, "The 'Motherless' Child: Some Issues in Adoption," *Psychiatric Times*, February 1, 2005.

Peter Jaret, "Saving Genia," *Health*, September 2004.

Tamara Jones, "The Price of Love," *Good Housekeeping*, September 2004.

Stephen A. Kapp, Thomas P. McDonald, and Kandi L. Diamond, "The Path to Adoption for Children of Color," *Child Abuse & Neglect*, February 2001.

Leslie Kaufman, "Cash Incentives for Adoptions Seen as Risk to Some Children," *New York Times*, October 29, 2003.

Garry Kranz, "Successful Adoption Programs Cost Little but Enhance Loyalty a Lot," *Workforce Management*, April 2004.

Marybeth Lambe, "A Love Beyond Measure," *Good Housekeeping*, January 2004.

Laurie Landry, "Grace's Adoption Story," *Chinese American Forum*, October 2002.

Michael A. Lipton and Barbara Sandler, "A Tug of War over Anna Mae He," *People*, March 29, 2004.

M. Therese Lysaught, "Embryo Adoption?" *Commonweal*, September 26, 2003.

Laurie C. Miller, "International Adoption: Infectious Diseases Issues," *Clinical Infectious Diseases*, January 15, 2005.

Amanda Paulson, "Adoption Parties: Caring or Cruel?" *Christian Science Monitor*, September 10, 2001.

Lisa Rauschart, "Not 'Unadoptable': New Effort to Find Homes for Older Foster Children," *World & I*, August 2004.

Scott D. Ryan, Sue Pearlmutter, and Victor Groza, "Coming Out of the Closet: Opening Agencies to Gay and Lesbian Adoptive Parents," *Social Work*, January 2004.

Eric Shedlow, "The Children's Revolution," *Community Care*, December 2, 2004.

Deborah H. Siegel, "Open Adoption of Infants: Adoptive Parents' Feelings Seven Years Later," *Social Work*, July 2003.

Jill Smolowe et al., "The Baby Chase," *People*, March 5, 2001.

Richard Tate, "The Battle to Be a Parent," *Advocate*, January 30, 2001.

Mark Whatley et al., "College Student Attitudes Toward Transracial Adoption," *College Student Journal*, September 2003.

Rosemary Zibart, "Teens Wanted: Adopt an Adolescent? Yes, There Are Families Crazy and Loving Enough to Take That On," *Time*, April 4, 2005.

INDEX